TWENTIETH CENTURY STUDIES

edited by

Donald Tyerman

NATIONALISM AND THE
INTERNATIONAL SYSTEM

Twentieth Century Studies

NATIONALISM AND THE INTERNATIONAL SYSTEM

by

F. H. HINSLEY

OCEANA PUBLICATIONS, INC.

DOBBS FERRY, N.Y.

Editor's Preface

Nationalism and the International System is the fifth in this series of Twentieth Century Studies. Each of them deals, in the way most appropriate to the subject, with a major theme of our changing times; all of them are concerned, distinctively, with the interplay of ideas and events, of events and ideas. Religion, economics, medicine and philosophy, and the place of these in twentieth century society, have been the subjects of the first four Studies;* education, literature and the role of war are among those next in train.

Wars are, of course, punctuation points in Professor Hinsley's own study of the integration of political communities, the consolidation of nation-states and the system of relations among them up to and after the two world wars. In earlier times civil violence and territorial wars flowed one into the other and were endemic. From the eighteenth century the nation-state had the power, and the technological means, to preserve the peace at home and to wage, or not wage, wars outside. Wars were larger, more destructive — and fewer. It was no longer hoped that perpetual peace could come by a return to Christendom or by an advance to some new, universal régime. The system that made the century from 1815 to 1914 predominantly a century of peace was the system of the balance of power among nation-states.

This is the system, and this the balance, that have been upset by the rise of new international powers in America, in Japan, in

---

* *Religion and Change* by David Edwards; *Economics and Policy* by Donald Winch; *The New Dimensions of Medicine* by Alan Norton; *Philosophy and Human Nature* by Kathleen Nott.

Russia and now in China; by the multiplication of new nation-states, in Africa as well as in Europe, in the East as well as in Latin America; and by the consummation of technological progress in nuclear weapons and their means of delivery. Professor Hinsley's Study goes directly as well as historically to the roots of this century's problem of peace and war—and survival.

There were some when the century began who looked to "inter-nationalism" to rectify the antagonisms of the "narrow nationalism" of the century before. Instead a peaceful century has been followed by two world wars and a peace kept for the past quarter of a century by the balance of deterrence between the weapons of the super-powers which could destroy the world several times over, while nations and tribes, continents and countries, states and provinces the world over are searching again, under the nuclear umbrella, for their identity—and their security. It is a vivid, graphic, contemporary picture, and a not unrelievedly pessimistic one, that emerges from this precise account and analysis of the nature of nationalism and the international system.

DONALD TYERMAN

Preface

Some of the following chapters are revised versions of the Lees-Knowles Lectures on Military Science delivered at Cambridge in the academical year 1970–1. I am grateful to the Master and Fellows of Trinity College, Cambridge, for inviting me to give the lectures. My thanks are also due to the University College of Wales, Aberystwyth, the rest of the book being an expansion of a paper the College invited me to give at a Conference held to commemorate the fiftieth anniversary of its establishment in 1919 of the Woodrow Wilson Professorship of International Politics.

April 1972

Contents

CHAPTER ONE

Introduction

Even among serious students of history and politics, nationalism continues to be a source of grave confusion.

Of the resulting disagreements some have revolved round the proposition that there is no such thing as nationalism, and that there never has been. These we may safely ignore: if nationalism has indeed been only an illusion or a myth, as some commentators would have it, it has at least been a persistent illusion and a powerful myth. So long, moreover, as words like "myth" and "illusion" continue to be applied to it, its persistence and its power as a state of mind will not be properly understood. Nationalism is—at least it rests upon—that way of thinking and feeling about one's political community which believes it is or ought to be a nation. The nation is one among a severely restricted number of possible political communities. When we add that for all men at all times there has been no choice but to belong to a political community, and that, for men who think and feel at all, there is no choice but to think and feel about this fundamental condition, if not necessarily to be active about it, we have perhaps said all that need be said by way of dismissing this proposition.

It must be admitted, however, that it was probably put forward in the first place—or, rather, as a last resort—only because other disagreements about nationalism have been so acute. Why it arises; how it has developed; whether it has been a reactionary or a revolutionary force; whether or not it has been the cause of such things as fascism, racism, imperialism and war—the debate on such issues has produced such inconclusive results as to make it a matter of no surprise that people should have sought escape from it by questioning the existence of nationalism itself.

The inconclusiveness of this debate might be illustrated by the literature on any of these questions during the last fifty years. It is particularly marked when what is concerned is the relation between nationalism and international developments, as we may show by considering how widely historians have differed about the role of nationalism in causing the catastrophe which has dominated the history of those years: the outbreak of the First World War.

For some historians, nationalism was the prime cause of war in 1914. This was Elie Halévy's view. Ever since the beginning of the century, he wrote, some forces had been making for revolution and others for war, but by 1914, powerful as were those making for revolution, which he summed up in the one word "socialism", the forces making for war were still more powerful. These he summed up in one phrase: "the principle of nationality". It was this principle that caused the Central Powers to take the awful responsibility of declaring war. If we ask why they did this,

> the answer should be: the rotten condition of the Austro-Hungarian Empire, the fact that the revolutionary principle of nationality was at work within its limits, and that it was about to break up into a number of independent states.[1]

That Halévy's view is still widely upheld will be sufficiently shown by this conclusion of Bernadotte Schmitt:

> The primary cause of the war was a conflict between political frontiers and the distribution of peoples, the denial of . . . the right of [national] self-determination . . . More than any other circumstance, this conflict between existing governments and their unhappy minorities was responsible for the catastrophe of 1914.[2]

[1] Halévy, E. (1930), *The World Crisis of 1914–18*, p. 37.
[2] Schmitt, B. E. (1958), *The Origins of the First World War*, pp. 6–7 (Historical Association).

Equally frequently, and sometimes just as positively, this verdict has been disputed. To Alfred Cobban the evidence suggested "that the half-century before 1914 witnessed rather a regression than a steady progress of the principle of self-determination, and that the outbreak of war in 1914 was due to the conflict of the great powers rather than to the strength of the movement for national self-determination".[1] And Vladimir Dedijer, the historian of Austria-Hungary's discontented nationalities, and particularly of the Young Bosnian movement which accomplished the Sarajevo assassination, has summed up in the same sense:

> To describe the Sarajevo assassination as either an underlying or an immediate cause of the 1914–18 War is to commit an enormity. It was an incident which under more normal international circumstances could not have provoked such momentous consequences . . . It was truly an unexpected gift . . . to the Viennese war party, which had sought, ever since the annexation crisis of 1908–9, a pretext for attacking Serbia, pacifying the South Slavs, and extending Habsburg power to the very gates of Salonika. Only in this sense were the South Slav national aspirations and colonial conditions of Bosnia and Hercegovina among the causes of the First World War . . .[2]

How are we to account for such total disagreement? It is not simply the outcome of subjective emotions. These might explain why Mr Dedijer, himself a Bosnian, should want to regard the Bosnian movement as having been merely the occasion for a war that was caused, not by nationalism, but by the clash of governments at a time when interstate relations were abnormally unstable. That Halévy took the opposite view from a keen anxiety to deflate the economic or materialist interpretation of the origins of the war is a conclusion that could be supported by several

[1] Cobban, A. (1969), *The Nation State and National Self-Determination*, p. 101.
[2] Dedijer, V. (London, 1966), *The Road to Sarajevo*, p. 445.

passages in his book.[1] But even if we do not dismiss these thoughts as uncharitable, we cannot extend them so far as to explain the disagreement between Professors Cobban and Schmitt. Nor may this, in its turn, be treated as being merely the result of different historiographical approaches or preoccupations, on the assumption that the student of diplomacy will explain in terms of diplomacy and the student of nationalism by calling in nationalism. It is Cobban, the historian of national self-determination, who prefers the clash of the Great Powers, Schmitt, the diplomatic historian, who relies on nationalism in the last resort.

In this last fact, on the other hand, we may perhaps have a clue to the correct explanation. Nationalism and the international behaviour of states are each of them complex subjects. It is difficult for a single historian or a single political scientist to be equally interested in, or conversant with, both. Add to this consideration the further fact that the greater a man's familiarity with the evidence, the greater, frequently, is his reluctance to advance firm conclusions on such stark issues as cause and effect, and a convincing answer to our question begins to emerge. What could be more understandable than that the diplomatic historian, still uncertain of the reasons for the outbreak of the First World War after devoting years to the study of diplomacy before 1914, should fall back on the *deus ex machina* of nationalism, of which his knowledge is far from complete? What more natural, again, than that the student of nationalism during those same years, acutely aware of the over-simplification involved in the argument that the war was caused by nationalism, should turn for his *deus ex machina* to

[1] The most striking of these are not his announcement that "I am no believer in the materialist conception of history" (p. 24) and his argument that "industrialism" was making for peace among the Great Powers but was defeated by "other forces, non-economic in their nature and stronger than industrialism" (p. 24). They are those where, having initially supposed that there might have been two sources of disequilibrium which men could not control — "the fact that one nation is found to have gained immensely in military or economic strength at the expense of the others; or that, within the limits of one or more nations, new nationalities have become self-conscious and wish to express themselves as independent states" (pp. 5–6) — he consistently ignored the first in his anxiety to show that war arose only out of the second. In fact, of course, he could just as easily have treated the first as the cause of war without disturbing his final conclusion that "man is not wholly made up of common sense and self-interest: such is his nature that he does not think life worth living if there is not something for which he is ready to lose his life" (p. 57).

a field which is less familiar to him—the clash of the Great Powers?

If this seems to be the reason for the unsatisfactory state of the controversy that still rages about nationalism and the origins of the First World War, it is not unlikely that it is the same procedure, or something very like it, which has confused the discussion of other questions involving the relationship of nationalism to the development of the international system. At least, this possibility is strong enough to justify an attempt to subject this relationship to a single analysis. But the real justification for this approach is to be found elsewhere. It does not lie in the need to bring together two separate fields of study so much as in the fact that nationalism and international conflict are inseparable, if different, facets of a single phenomenon—of the division of men into political groups.

The nature and the history of nationalism are partly explained by the processes of clash and collaboration within the body-politic, but also by the processes of clash and collaboration between bodies-politic. The development of an international system has involved changes in the character of relations between bodies-politic. But these changes have themselves reflected changes in the character of the bodies-politic, and these further changes are intimately linked with the nature and history of nationalism. Unless we recognise this—so long as we continue to think of them as being, not two sides of the same problem, but separate if inter-locking issues—the connection between nationalism and inter-national relations cannot cease to be a matter of subjective interpretation, if not of prejudiced judgments.

It is not to be hoped that, as a result of treating them as two sides of a single problem, we shall succeed in ending all contro-versy about these subjects. But this approach may assist us to return to first principles for a definition of nationalism and to resort to a wider perspective when reconstructing the history of international relations; and by these means we may be able to clear away a part of the prevailing confusion.

PART I : NATIONALISM

CHAPTER TWO

The Bases of Nationalism

Nationalism has been defined as that state of mind in which the political loyalty is felt to be owed to the nation. This definition has its short-comings. Before we turn to them we should note that it has one great virtue.

It does not assume that, when nationalism comes to exist where it has not existed before, it does so because men have discovered a political loyalty which they previously lacked. On the contrary, it implies that men have then transferred to the nation the political loyalty which they previously gave to some other structure— that what has changed is not the quality of this loyalty but the object on which it is showered or the vehicle through which it is expressed. And all the evidence is in favour of this implication.

There is, in the first place, the probability that in men the political loyalty—the need to be devoted to some political community, whatever the form of that community may be—is an ancient, if not even an innate, attribute. This probability is supported by all we know about the differences between human societies and groups in other species. "Human societies generally devise methods of separating groups—which we may call . . . tribes—and of giving them a formal character and a binding unity." "The unity of the human tribe is evidently sustained by all the barriers which separate it from other tribes . . . The mental evolution of men has therefore carried with it a growth of tribal feeling which is one of the properties which set him apart from his animal ancestors."[1]

Less debatable, as they are based on our knowledge of human

[1] Darlington, C. D. (London, 1969), *The Evolution of Man in Society*, pp. 57–8.

societies in historical times, are two other considerations which point in the same direction. Until comparatively recently the community to which men felt they owed their political loyalty was not the nation. This was not because the idea of the nation did not yet exist, but because the political loyalty was everywhere commanded by some other form of community.

As an ethnic or cultural group the nation, like the family, the clan, the tribe and other ethnic and cultural groups, is primordial: the earliest extant texts in Hittite, Vedic Sanskrit and Mycenean Greek all contain a word for it.[1] And the Romans were following all earlier usage when they pronounced the Jews to be a *natio*, as also the Greeks and the assemblage of German tribes, because it was not as Jews, Greeks or Germans that they were politically organised. In the same way, they did not regard themselves, the Romans, as a *natio*, precisely because they were politically organised as tribes, as a city-state or as an empire, on lines that made the word irrelevant to them.

In Europe the word for and the idea of the nation retained their Roman or non-political sense during most of the Middle Ages, if not for longer still. Occasionally—though this is more common beyond Europe—they do so to this day. Later on, in connection with the need to define the nation, we shall have to consider in some detail the process by which they lost it. For the moment it is sufficient to say that what we know about this process—about the politicisation of the nation or the emergence of the nation as the political community—provides further support for the view that nationalism is but one form of the basic political loyalty which may be expressed in other ways than in loyalty to the nation—in attachment to the clan, the tribe, the city-state, the empire.

It does so by revealing that the process has by no means in- variably consisted of the awakening to political consciousness of a pre-existing but non-political sense of being a nation. Many factors besides this have contributed to it—geography; habit and the passage of time; conquest and the impact of strong govern- ment; resistance to conquest and government—and men have sometimes invented political nations where, as was the case with

[1] Beneviste, E. (Paris, 1969), *Le Vocabulaire des Institutions Indo-Européennes*.

the Swiss, no ethnic, cultural or linguistic nation existed. Among
the Scots in Scotland, on the other hand, the sense of being a
nation culturally remains lively after 250 years during which
most of them have attached their political loyalty to the political
nation of Great Britain. None of these factors, in other words, not
even the pre-existing sense of being a nation culturally, ethnically
or linguistically, has been sufficient to ensure that a political
nation will be formed.

We may safely conclude, indeed, that while any or all of these
factors may have influenced the timing of the process and the con-
formation of its end-result, the only consideration that has been
essential for the emergence of the political nation has been the
fact that the need to belong to some political community
takes on the national dimension—assumes that the political
community is or ought to be the nation—when circumstances
make this possible and in whatever way the circumstances make
appropriate.

Before we accept that the basis of nationalism is the political
loyalty which in no way differs from the political loyalty that may
devote itself to other structures than the nation—to the clan, the
tribe, the city-state or the empire—we should note that it is
possible to object to this conclusion.

We cannot invalidate it by arguing that not only has the dimension or the vehicle of this loyalty varied, but also its intensity, and
that nationalism has differed from the other possible expressions
of it in that the loyalty has been more intense when the vehicle has
been the nation than when it has been some other political structure. The evidence is overwhelming that the clan, the tribe, the
city-state or the empire have mobilised the political loyalty no less
effectively and intensely than the nation has done, and perhaps
even more so. It is equally undeniable, however, that when it has
been associated with the nation, no less than when it has been
associated with the clan, the tribe or the empire, the political
loyalty has expressed itself more intensely at some times and places
than at others, and this fact prompts an objection which we cannot
neglect.

We may for this reason use the word "nationalism" in two different senses. As in the conclusion that we are examining, we may make it stand for the general condition in which the political loyalty has been nationalised — has entered the national as distinct from some other stage. Or we may confine it to those more particular situations in which the nationalised political loyalty has assumed its more intense or extreme or even excessive forms. And if we do so confine it, we must reject the conclusion. Instead of defining nationalism as the nationalised stage of the basic political loyalty, we then define it as a special stage within that stage.

In the literature on nationalism there has been a strong tendency to adopt the second of these usages. On the principle that we should use words as they are commonly used, it might be argued that we should conform to it. But on the principle that in our use of words we should as far as possible avoid causing confusion, we must recognise that it has its drawbacks. One of them is terminological. If we adopt this usage, what word shall we use for the "normal" or restrained expression of the national political loyalty? "Nationality" and "patriotism" have both been pressed into service. But we need the word "nationality" for another purpose — to mean that sense or sentiment of being a nation ethnically, culturally or linguistically which undoubtedly can exist before the political loyalty is nationalised. Patriotism, again, is commonly given a different application: we use it when we speak of the political loyalty being attached to any community, whatever the form of the community may be. On the other hand we have other words, more specific than nationalism, which are more appropriate for describing the national political loyalty when it is inflamed: "chauvinism", "zenophobia", even "fascism".

As the mention of these words should serve to warn us, the restricted usage may lead to confusion in a second direction. If we equate nationalism with only intense or extreme expressions of the national loyalty, we obscure what it is that fundamentally distinguishes the national political loyalty. This is the fact that it is devoted to the nation as distinct from some other political structure. If, on the other hand, we equate it with the national stage of the political loyalty, without regard to the different degrees of intensity which it may assume when it is in that stage, we shall not only preserve this fundamental distinction. We shall also be working with the definition which enables us to explain why it is that it is just when the national political loyalty is most extreme that it is ceasing to be national. This is the fact that, as we shall see later on, it is then that it is moving from the national into another of the stages—the tribal, the imperial—between which the political loyalty may easily oscillate.

For these reasons it seems preferable to give the word the wider of these two meanings. Nationalism may be muted or acute, active or inactive, articulate or taken for granted. But we shall be wise to insist that its basis, or one of its bases, is the association of the political loyalty with the nation, as distinct from any other political community—that it is indeed the state of mind in which the political loyalty is felt to be owed to the nation.

If this is accepted, then its other basis must consist of whatever it is that distinguishes the nation as a political structure from other political structures. What does distinguish it? By what process, again, does the nation replace other structures as the political group? When we ask these questions we begin to see where the definition is inadequate. While it emphasises, rightly, that nationalism expresses the political sentiment which may be expressed in other ways than in loyalty to the nation, it stops short of defining the nation.

Attempts to remedy this deficiency have commonly supposed that the criteria of the nation as a political group or a political concept have been unvarying through time and space. This is the approach of those who claim that the origin of the political nation dates back to the fifteenth and sixteenth centuries when the consolidation of the territorial state completed, if only in Europe, the destruction of the Middle Ages. The same approach is adopted, however, by those who insist that even in Europe it goes back only to various dates at the end of the eighteenth century or the beginning of the nineteenth, on the ground that it was not until then that men came to think of the nation as the overriding cultural community and to believe that each such community possessed, or ought to possess, its own state. Nor do these two views merely conflict with one another in consequence of being based on different criteria. As soon as we apply them to the history of Europe we discover that each is untenable because its definition of the political nation is too arbitrary.

The first confines to the sixteenth century what was a development partly of the Middle Ages and partly of later years. Not even in the sixteenth century, moreover, was the territorial state the only force contributing to the rise of the political nation. The second not only ignores all developments before the eighteenth century but also fails to accommodate much of the subsequent history of nationalism. And so much is this so that it is necessary to adopt another approach: to accept that the political nation has been neither fixed nor simple in form or as an idea, and to recognise that the problem is to explain the limits within which its character has varied through time and from place to place.

To understand nationalism we must recognise that two kinds of movement have to be taken into account. There is, first, the line of progression along which the basic political loyalty shifts from the stage of the clan, the tribe, the collection of tribes, the city-state, or the empire to that of the nation. And then, within the national stage of that progression, there is a second kind of movement—that by which the structure and the conception of the political nation are themselves subjected to change.

CHAPTER THREE

The Movement of the Political Loyalty into the National Stage

What considerations, we must next ask, have produced and regulated the first of these two movements: the movement of the political loyalty into the national stage?

In order to answer this question we must make two points about the nature of the political community. The first is that a community is a political community only when the relations between its government and its society, the two elements of which it is composed, are the relations of ruler and ruled. It is true that we do not always use the term political in this sense. We apply it more widely to the dialogue or process of argument and competition that goes on both in political communities and in many organisations which, though they have both membership and government of a sort, are not political communities. Thus, of a college or a tennis club or a political party we talk of the politics or the political activity involved in governing it. We know, however, that it is not a political community and that its government is not political government in the stricter sense of the word which requires the members to be ruled by a government which has, by force or consent or a mixture of both, the authority to exercise rule over them.

The second point concerns the method of distinguishing between types of political community. In different contexts, for different purposes, these have been distinguished from each other in various ways. For our purpose, however, the fundamental fact is that, historically, they have been divided in terms of the relations between their society and their government, that is in terms of the nature of rule, into one of two categories—those ruled by non-state or pre-state government and those ruled by the state.

This categorisation will be rejected—at least there will be some difficulty in accepting it—because the term "state", like the term "political", has come to be used ambiguously. To use it in the precise sense that equates it with one category of political government, in order to distinguish that from non-state or pre-state types of political government, is to go against a strong tradition by which the term has been applied to all types of political rule. But it is the tradition which causes confusion, not this distinction. There are non-state or pre-state types of political rule, and the difference between them and the state is no less marked than that between political government, whatever the type, and the non-political government of communities which are not political communities.

What is this difference? We have said already that it is dictated by the relationship between the society and the government of the political community. To emphasise that it is thus fundamental, and also to avoid a further possible source of confusion, we must add that it has nothing to do, at any rate directly, with those other distinctions that we find it necessary to draw between forms of government in other contexts. The non-state or pre-state type of rule has been exercised by government that was monarchical or aristocratic or democratic in form, just as there have been monarchical, aristocratic and democratic states. Non-state or pre-state political rule, again, may be justified arbitrarily by absolutist or even theocratic claims to authority, but the government exercising it may equally be limited in its claims. Similarly, the bureaucratised modern democratic state is only one of the forms of government that have exercised the state type of rule, which may also be wielded by a divine-right individual or an absolutist narrow group. For what distinguishes it, even at its most primitive stage of development, from non-state or pre-state political rule, even when that is complex and sophisticated, is simply its method of rule. While in the non-state type of rule the emphasis is the other way about, the state type of rule places the emphasis on ruling territory, rather than on ruling social groups; and its method of rule, regardless of the origin and basis of its authority, is administrative.

The distinction may be illustrated at the level of local government. In both types of political rule the government rules the community ultimately, but in neither case can it rule without devolving some of its power. What distinguishes the state from pre-state or non-state types of rule is not the extent of the devolution—for the state may be more decentralised than pre-state or non-state government even if it is normally less so—but the principle on which it tries to make the devolution rest. In non-state political communities local power resides in indigenous local authorities which recognise the headship of the centre. With the state it is otherwise. It confers local power on authorities which, indigenous or not, exercise it as its agents; and not the least obstacle to be overcome in the slow rise of the state has been the difficulty it has had in getting this principle accepted.

When we turn from this illustration to study the circumstances in which the state has succeeded in this task, and has brought its type of rule into existence, we may understand why it diverges in the way we have described from non-state or pre-state types of rule. In a political community which is confined to an un-differentiated social group, or to closely related social groups, a non-state or a pre-state type of government—non-administrative institutions and procedures, embedded in social custom and scarcely diverging from it—is sufficient. Whatever the power it may wield, however complex it may become, government in these circumstances has no call to adopt the administrative style of the state. The state's administrative style becomes indispens-able, on the other hand, when social groups within the same territory become so differentiated, as a result of economic activity or cultural mixture or the conquest by one group of the territory of another, that it is only by emphasising that rule is government over territory that different social groups can be held together in a single political community.

It is not too much to say, indeed, that in the last resort the political community may be organised around one of two conflicting principles. These are not the social principle and the government principle. All societies which are also political communities have government in the strict sense of the word "political": they are ruled. The conflicting principles are the social principle and the state principle, and they are reflected in the two basic types of rule—the non-state or pre-state, which rules in conformity with the social principle, and the state which, at least initially, seeks to supersede it.

If this is the key to the origin and nature of the state, the rise of the state is in its turn the key to the movement of the political loyalty into the national stage.

The clan, the tribe, the collection of tribes, even the "city-state"—when they are political communities, these are political communities in which the composition of society has not yet become so mixed as to produce the administrative principle of rule that goes with the state, and in which this principle has not been imposed by a state from outside. Hence the nature of the city-state. Whether in its antique or its modern form, this is properly regarded as a collection of closely related clans or tribes at its most sophisticated level of development—that at which the refinement and the professionalisation of methods of rule have developed as far as is compatible with its inability, on account of its social cohesion, to produce the distinction between society and government which is the *raison d'être* of the state. Hence, again, the tendency of collections of tribes to subdivide as they enlarge and become socially more complicated, rather than perpetuate a level of inter-mixture which has begun to require the transition to the state. The clan, the tribe, the collection of tribes, the city-state are also political communities in which the political loyalty, though it may be intense, is not a national political loyalty.

On the ground that the political loyalty must of course remain non-national or pre-national when the political community is non-national or pre-national, we could argue that there is no connection between these two characteristics, or none but a coincidental one. There is, however, an intimate connection between the rise of the state and the transition of the political community from the pre-national to the national stage, and we are justified in saying that it is not until the victory of the administrative over the social principle as the basis of rule has resulted in, or has resulted from, the interposition of the state that the political loyalty, also, enters the national stage.

It does so in a political community that is usually more extensive and less cohesive than its pre-national forerunner. But this is not all. Not even after the state has come into existence have the political community and the political loyalty easily or even necessarily become national. Historically, either there has been an immense delay between the emergence of the state in a political community and the first stirrings there of nationalism — of national consciousness in its political form — or the emergence of the state has not been followed at all by this further development. The victory of the state, a necessary condition of nationalism, has not been a sufficient condition of it. And in order to see why it has not been so, we must introduce the problem of empire and understand the close association that has existed between empire and the rise of the state.

This association is obvious enough when, as has probably been most commonly the case throughout history, pre-state communities have acquired the state by having it imposed on them in the wake of their conquest by other communities. But it follows from the nature and function of the state that in the only definition of empire that is universally valid — the rule of one government over more than one social group — the state has begun as an empire even when, less commonly, the collection of tribes or the city has generated the state for itself, from its need to adjust to the increasing mixture of its cultural composition or because of the widening of its class differences or in its search for defence against the imperialism of neighbouring states.[1] In either case it has been the work of the state to bring about new

---

[1] On these alternatives to conquest as the origins of the state see Darlington, *Evolution of Man*, pp. 210ff., and d'Entrèves, A. P., *The Notion of the State* pp. 153ff.

relations in society by amalgamating diverse social groups, assimilating recalcitrant populations and standardising, or at least reconciling, languages, laws and customs in the territorial area of its rule.

In either case, on the other hand—in relation to the communities on which it has been immediately based, no less than in relation to outlying communities which it has treated more openly as conquests—the state has remained imperial in its attitude to rule until it has been enabled by the passage of time to compromise with the society in which it governs—and forced to do so by the strength of resistance to it. For the resistance of the social community to the assimilating or imperialising work of the state has usually been so great that it is this which has played the largest part in gradually de-imperialising the forms and attitudes of the state.[1]

The political nation, we may say, and the sense of belonging to a political nation, have thus emerged within the framework laid down by the state. They have done so after a more or less lengthy adjustment between the state and the non-state or pre-state political communities on which that framework has been imposed. The political community and the political loyalty have become national only when, in relation to the political community which has acquired the state, the state has developed beyond being an empire—than which the nation is usually less extensive and more cohesive.

Two objections might be made to this analysis.

It might be said, in the first place, that, in those situations where communities have, in our phrase, generated the state for themselves, it is questionable whether the word "imperial" should be applied even to the initial stages of the work of the state. And it is certainly true that in these cases the process of compromise by the state with the community has begun early and

---

[1] For a statement of this process, as reflected in the development of law from the law of power, based on fear by the ruled and force and self-legitimation by the ruler, to the normally self-executing law of reciprocity or co-ordination, based on self-interest, a sense of duty and consensual legitimation of authority, see Schwarzenberger, G. (London, 1971), *International Law and Order*, pp. 12–15.

been most marked. Thus it is noticeable that such states have usually been confederal in form. The Swiss union, a state formed during the thirteenth and fourteenth centuries out of alliances between diverse communities in the search for security against external imperial encroachment, is one example. Other examples are provided by the origins of the Dutch republic and, later still, by the beginnings of the United States of America.

Even if this objection were allowed, however, it would not be fatal to the argument we have advanced. It would commit us only to accepting that the state may sometimes do its centralising administrative work in ways which are not imperialist, or for which the word "empire" is not an appropriate term. And this we may easily do. For even when states have been established in a population which has not previously been ruled by a state, or have been established in defence against an empire rather than being imperialist themselves, the tortured early history of their relations with their populations still goes to show that their emergence has at least ushered in a long struggle between the social and the administrative principles of rule.

The second objection has more serious implications for the argument that the political loyalty has not entered upon the national stage until the state has succeeded in this struggle and has established the administrative principle of rule. It is the objection that the sense of being a nation politically has sometimes preceded the formation of the state or even been instrumental in creating it — that at least in recent times, if not in the case of the Swiss union, the Dutch republic or the United States, and perhaps even in those earlier situations also, a nationalist movement based on the existence of a national political consciousness within a society has sometimes created the state. But before we accept this argument we must bear three things in mind.

While nationalist movements are always expressions of the resistance of the social principle to the state principle, we must remember, first, that not all such resistance movements have been nationalist movements. They may be anti-nationalist in that they seek to preserve provincial and tribal ways which exclude or have priority even over the sense of nationality. Even if they seek to preserve the ways, the culture, of a nation they may still be expressions of the sense of nationality without being nationalist.[1] Although it is undertaken on behalf of a nation, the distinguishing feature of a nationalist movement is that it is based on the sense of being a political nation, and the essential test that it is so based is that it aims to turn the nation into a political nation by providing it with its own state. Rebellion, separatism, constitutional argument may thus be inseparable from it. But nationalism would be denuded of all its meaning if we did not carefully distinguish nationalist movements from constitutional struggles, separatist revolts and tribal rebellions.

The second point arises when we reflect on those movements which have been truly nationalist by this test. Not only have they been formed in resistance to an existing state, but also they have been nationalist because, and to the extent that, the existing state has produced by its centralising and assimilating influence, or at least by its example, the social and intellectual conditions in which opposition to its work can be motivated by the essential demand of nationalism.

And what if this demand—the demand that the nation must have its own state—is satisfied? A third point now becomes relevant. If nationalist movements have been nationalist only when the work of an existing state has been sufficiently advanced to make them so, they have usually succeeded only when that state has been far from completing the assimilation of the breakaway populations. On this account, while the sense of being a distinctive political nation may have been the mainspring of the successful opposition to the state, it has been confined to limited social circles, and much of the opposition has consisted of the pooling of more local and non-nationalist separatisms. The new state has thus not only been loosely confederal in form, to

[1] As is illustrated by the following exchange in the year 1848:
"What do you understand by 'nation'?" inquired Kossuth.
"A race which possesses its own language, customs and culture", was the Serb reply, "and enough self-consciousness to preserve them."
"A nation must also have its own government," objected Kossuth.
"We do not go so far," Kostik explained; "the nation can live under several different governments, and again several nations can form a single state." See Smith, A. D. (London, 1971), *Theories of Nationalism*, quoting from Seton-Watson (London, 1911), *The Southern Slav Question and the Habsburg Monarchy*.

suit the diversity of its several communities; it has also found
that, within those communities, the sense of being a political
nation remains limited to a minority until the new state has in its
turn made progress in assimilating and nationalising them. Not
infrequently, moreover, it has found that it cannot make this
progress unless it is as imperialist in its rule as the state which it
has replaced.

These points are all borne out, as has already been suggested,
by the early history of the Swiss Union, the Dutch republic and
the United States of America. The third point is especially
underlined by more recent experience elsewhere. The state in
Yugoslavia, for example, originated in resistance to, successively,
the centralisation of the state of Austria-Hungary, the expansion
of the state of Serbia, and conquest by Hitler's empire. But just
as it has always been a loose federation because its establishment
was preceded and assisted by no widespread sense of Yugoslav
nationalism, so the extent to which it has failed to generate such a
nationalism is revealed by the fact that it is now a multi-
national state which is seeking to stabilise itself as such by converting from a federation into "a sovereign state of six sovereign
republics" or "a commune of six republics and two autonomous
regions". Some of the republics are indeed resisting even this
formula as being too "unitarist". Among the Croatians, particularly, there is a demand for full autonomy for the Croatian
Republic. In the Serbian Republic the considerable Albanian
population is pressing for the creation of a separate Albanian
Republic within the Yugoslav state.

In the light of these facts we must somewhat modify the old
definition of a federal state as a unitary state in the process of
formation or dissolution: although Yugoslavia has never been a
unitary state, it remains an open question whether the federation
can itself survive, and eventually create a Yugoslav nationalism,
if it is diluted to the extent demanded by its component nationalisms. But we need not modify our general conclusion about the
movement of the political loyalty into the national stage.

Even when the state is the product of a successful nationalist
movement on behalf of a nation against another state, and not only

3

when a state produces a nation, the idea of the political nation, which cannot emerge so long as a society evades the rule of the state, still cannot be realised in practice until a society, having undergone the territorial rule of the state, and a state, having modified the imperial style that initially goes with such rule, have together come to the end of the imperial phase of their relations.

CHAPTER FOUR

Concepts of the Nation

The foregoing analysis explains the nationalisation of the political loyalty—its movement into the national stage—in terms of the mutual interaction of a society and a state. Whenever this movement has taken place it has been because, in a society which has undergone the rule of a state, one of two conditions has obtained. Either the society and the state have so far adjusted to each other as to produce a political nation, or else their failure to do so has produced in a part of the society the wish to establish a different state. Whenever, conversely, these conditions have obtained, the movement has taken place.

It might be felt that we should next explain why, sometimes as a result of co-operation between a state and a society and sometimes as a result of opposition between them, this movement has taken place at different times in different political societies—in Europe from the fourteenth and fifteenth centuries; in Japan, Thailand, Burma and Persia from the sixteenth and seventeenth centuries; in the New World from the time of the American Revolution; in other areas beyond Europe in the nineteenth century or, even, only in our own day. In fact, we could scarcely answer this question without undertaking a survey of universal history, and such a survey would throw little further light on nationalism.

It would confirm that throughout modern times the tendency for political communities to evolve into political nations, or to wish to do so, has been universal and persistent. As to why they have done so at different times, however, it would show no more than that they have done so when, either in the wake of their development towards greater social and political complexity or from the urge towards more rapid social and political advance, they have reached the point when sufficient proportions of their populations have felt that no group other than the nation can command their political loyalty. Nor would it assist to make a detailed investigation of the forces — economic and communications growth; industrialisation or the wish for industrialisation; modernisation or the wish for modernisation; international rivalry — which have accompanied the movement of political communities to this point. These have formed the context in which the political loyalty has moved into the national stage, as the political dialogue between a society and a state has constituted the mechanism which has moved it. But instead of illuminating nationalism, the study of them will impede our understanding of it unless we recognise that the crucial problem lies elsewhere.

For it is not only the case that the political loyalty has moved into the national stage at different times in different communities. According to when and in what circumstances it has so moved, it has attached itself to different conceptions of what constitutes the political nation. Nor is this all. Within the community which has in fact become a political nation the conception of the political nation has changed from time to time. Within what limits, and why, has the conception of the political nation varied from time to time and from place to place? This is the question we must answer if we are to understand the changes that have occurred, and that may occur, in the character and the intensity of nationalism.

We may begin the answer by referring back to our analysis of the movement of the political loyalty into the national stage. If that analysis is correct, it follows, from the importance it attached to the part played by the relations between a state and a society, that conceptions of the political nation should have varied and moved between two extremes. At one extreme they should have emphasised criteria associated with and advanced by the state; at the other, criteria associated with and advanced by the political community as a society. On the other hand, we should expect to find that, though differently emphasised, both state criteria and social criteria have been incorporated in every conception. When a conception of the nation has been based heavily on social criteria, and advanced by a society in resistance to a state, it has still demanded that the nation should have its own state, even as conceptions of the nation advanced by the state, and stressing the state's criteria, have nevertheless been concerned with the nation as a social community. In the discussion of nations as political structures it is often urged that "there are culture-nations and state-nations" — political nations based on social criteria and political nations based on state criteria. Whenever this proposition is put to the test, it has to be conceded that "we have always to keep clearly in mind that in historical reality these different forms merge into one another".[1] We should expect to find that the same has been true of conceptions of the political nation.

Even so, according to the relationship between a state and a society at the time when they were advanced, some will have placed the chief stress on the criteria associated with the state and others on the criteria associated with the political community.

We shall often encounter another complication when we consider their range and development. We should not be surprised if the criteria underlying them have also changed with changing circumstances, from time to time and from place to place. State criteria of what constitutes the political nation will have reflected the character of the state, and of assumptions about it. It is unlikely that they were the same at the time of the French Revolution as they were for sixteenth-century monarchs, or as they are in the minds of African presidents in the twentieth century. The same is true of the criteria associated with the community as a society. We have no choice but to refer to them in general terms as "social" or "cultural". But this is not because a society or the culture of a society is made up of many elements — customs, myths, institutions, history, law, religion, language, even race — so much as because social or cultural definitions of political nationhood will thus have been able to select from and to emphasise these different elements in different ways in different societies, as conditions have required.

[1] Meinecke, F. (1922 edn), *Weltbürgertum und Nationalstaat*, p. 15.

The earliest conception of the political nation was that which appears to have been common to the "state-nations" which emerged in Europe during the fourteenth, fifteenth and sixteenth centuries and elsewhere — in Japan, Thailand, Burma and Persia most prominently — during the seventeenth and eighteenth centuries.

These "state-nations" emerged in areas where the state had long been engaged in the work of territorial consolidation and social assimilation. It was the progress made in this work which had at last stirred the communities underlying each state to value the possession of common political institutions and of shared political traditions to the extent that they felt themselves to be a political nation. We might thus expect their conception of the nation to have been largely, if not wholly, based on the governmental and territorial criteria of the state. In fact it gave almost as much prominence to the social criteria of common language and religion.

This striking fact arose from the circumstances in which the state had made its contribution to the formation of these early political nations. By establishing a common government and administration over several communities, and by thus quickening social mobility and economic activity within and between them, the state had indeed created the framework and the integration without which the sense of being a political nation could not have developed. But it had not created the political loyalty that was another pre-condition of the political nation.

The sentiment had pre-existed, but hitherto it had been distributed between two poles — between the primordial but intensely political feeling of belonging to a community of local or provincial scale, and the primordial but non-political idea of belonging to a cultural or social nation of wider expanse. The framework created by the state enabled the two poles to be connected in such a way that these two forms of sentiment could flow into each other and produce the loyalty of political nationality. The process had its parallel in the development of language. In Europe, for example, it was just at the time when the non-provincial Latin or French, which had hitherto fixed a gulf between rulers and ruled, were yielding to the vernaculars, that the provincial vernaculars were themselves being consolidated into vernaculars of a wider, national range.

If it was for this reason that society was no less influential than the state in providing the criteria and shaping the concept of the earliest political nations, it was for the same reason that the sentiment of being a nation in the political sense continued to be fitful in the early stages. It could be intense in some circumstances. In others, because it was still confined to small sections of the populations, and because even there it was liable to be submerged when competing with the political loyalties which still attached to clan or province or church, it could fade or disappear. And all the more was this the case because in the process of fusion or merger which we have just described—in the course of the politicisation of the idea of the nation and of the nationalisation of the political group—the state nowhere found it easy to move away from imperialism in its forms and outlooks.

During the sixteenth and seventeenth centuries, accordingly, much of the resistance to its standardising and centralising work continued to be inspired by the old political loyalties, non-national and trans-national, of locality and church. As this work went on, however, a new phenomenon appeared: national political opposition to the continuing autocratic and dynastic style of the state's administration and rule. When we study the resulting increase of conflict within the political communities it is never easy to decide which of its sources, the old and the new, was uppermost, so often were they intermingled in a single struggle. It may be suggested, however, that to investigate these struggles with an eye to discovering the varying degrees to which, instead of seeking merely to avoid assimilation by a state, they centred on the attempt to join another state, or to create a new state, or to take over the existing state and modify its established imperial outlooks and forms, would be the best way of estimating how far the idea of the political nation had progressed, and within which territorial institutional frames, in the different areas.

As these internal struggles varied in their content and make-up, so they differed in their outcome. Here it was the strengthening of absolutism, there the establishment of republican forms, elsewhere the rise of mixed or parliamentary monarchies. Whatever the outcome, however, there was a general movement throughout Europe from the second half of the seventeenth century towards the establishment of internal political stability on the basis of reconciliation between the community and the state.

Even in republican regimes the social elements which had acquired control of the state came to terms in the course of exercising its powers with the inescapable need to adopt its administrative style. Even in the most retrograde of the autocratic monarchies the state cast its harsh skin of despotism and imperialism in a process of re-adjustment to social developments within the territory which it ruled. During the next hundred years the European states, regardless of their form of government, increasingly became more anchored to, or national in, the communities which they already governed even if, regardless of their form of government, they remained as expansionist or as imperialist as they had ever been in their attitude to outlying communities both within Europe and, increasingly, beyond it — as interested as ever in adding yet further communities by marriage, merger and war to those inside their territorial and institutional frameworks, which they were now consolidating at a rapid rate.

The process of reconciliation owed much to the quickening of economic activity and social mobility in the communities that were being consolidated. It owed still more to the expanding capacities and functions of the state. On the one hand, increasingly complex societies were needing more regulation by government. On the other, more complex state machines were evolving, the better able to provide it, as a result of the percolation of the scientific revolution from the study to the government office and the overflow of a growing movement of technological and methodological innovation from economic activity into the administrative and the political fields. It was not for nothing that the political ideology which was the counterpart to this intellectual, technological and methodological advance emphasised the merits and the possibilities of the characteristic function of the state.

For forms of government let fools contest;
Whate'er is best administered is best.

Pope's couplet summed up what had come to be the principal
political belief throughout Europe by the beginning of the
Enlightenment of the eighteenth century.

Not surprisingly, again, the rise of this belief combined with the
actual growth in the power and functions of the state to produce a
change in the concept of the nation. What now took place was not
the first emergence of the nation as a political concept but a steady
shift away from cultural and social criteria in the definition of the
political nation towards the definition of the political nation in territorial and institutional terms. By the beginning of the eighteenth
century, while they could not be wholly eliminated, the cultural
and social elements in the concept of the political nation were
everywhere in Europe beginning to be submerged. Most of the
territorial bodies-politic still comprised diverse cultural and social
communities, though some were culturally and socially more
uniform than others. In all the territorial bodies-politic, however,
cultural, social and even linguistic uniformity was ceasing to be
important for the sense of being a nation, and the sole test of
nationhood was coming to be possession by and submission to a
territorial, administrative state.

This development was not confined to the views of those who
ruled the state. Where it was accompanied by the growth of constitutional rights and democratic ideas, these themselves were
also advanced within the framework of the territorial and institutional conception of the nation. The most eloquent illustration of this fact is provided by the rise of populist theories
during the seventeenth century. Basing themselves on the Contract
theory of government, they came to share this conception of the
nation.

Before and during the struggles between governments and communities of the sixteenth and seventeenth centuries, this theory had
been used to defend religious minorities, separatist elements
(notably the Church and the aristocracy), and particularist communities against the centralising state. It was one of the outcomes

of those struggles that by the end of the seventeenth century, in Hobbes's version of it, it had come to be one of the main justifications of the authority of the state. On the other hand, it had also established itself by then in a constitutionalist form as the dominant doctrine for the defence against the state of the rights of the people conceived of as a nation. But in its constitutionalist, no less than in its authoritarian, version, it unhesitatingly maintained, in Locke's words of the 1680s, that "whenever any number of men so unite into one society as to quit every one his executive power of the Law of Nature, and to resign it to the public, there and there only is a political or civil society". For constitutionalist no less than for authoritarian thinkers the one factor which made a community of individuals into a people or a nation was their agreement to set up a common government, even if constitutionalists also insisted that government must incorporate a common legislature.[1]

During the last third of the eighteenth century the economic and social quickening of some of Europe's societies attained to such dimensions as to produce the first modern agrarian and industrial revolutions. Partly on this account, and partly because the states again found it difficult to adjust their attitudes and procedures to the increased rate of change, the ideology of the Enlightenment was overwhelmed in the wave of intellectual and political discontent which culminated in the American and the French

---

[1] The dominance acquired by the territorial and institutional concept of the nation is further illustrated by the way in which governments now reacted to their recognition that, with the spread of constitutional ideas, the principle of nationality was becoming a political issue. Up to the end of the seventeenth century the inhabitants of conquered territory became subjects of the state to which it was ceded. Thereafter the practice developed of allowing them to retain their original nationality, or to choose a new nationality, if they would leave the ceded territory. Perhaps the earliest occasion on which the permission was granted was the Treaty of Limerick of 1691, which gave all the inhabitants of Ireland the right to be shipped to France with their belongings at the expense of their conqueror, William of Orange. See O'Higgins, P. (1969), "The Treaty of Limerick, 1691", *Grotian Society Papers*, pp. 212–32 . When Strasbourg was transferred to France in 1697 this precedent was followed. See Lawrence, T. J. (1925), *The Principles of International Law*, pp. 92–3. During the eighteenth century such a stipulation became a regular part of treaties of cession. Thus the Treaty of Paris of 1763 declared the inhabitants of Great Britain's conquests in French Canada to be British subjects, but conceded that "they shall have the right to withdraw within eighteen months". See Parry, Clive (1957), *Nationality and Citizenship Laws of the Commonwealth*, Vol. I, p. 481.

Revolutions. At the same time, a new concept of the political nation was formulated to rival the one that had prevailed for the past 100 years. The institutional and territorial concept of the political nation, as defined by the work and the frontiers of the state, was now challenged by the conviction that the political nation ought to be co-ordinate with a distinctive cultural, ethnic or linguistic community—that the territorial limits of states ought to coincide with areas that were ethnically, culturally and linguistically uniform.

Not unnaturally, in view of this coincidence, it is commonly believed that the rise of the social definition of the political nation in its modern form, with its cultural, ethnic and linguistic criteria, was the necessary outcome of the movement in the western societies towards the democratisation of the state. Neither the demands of logic nor the facts of history support this view. In logic, the territorial and institutional concept of the nation was perfectly compatible with the democratisation movement, which indeed stressed the equality of all citizens rather than the need to discriminate between men on the basis of culture or language. As for the historical facts, the evidence is overwhelming that the men who made the American and the French revolutions adhered to the established territorial and institutional criteria of the nation, and necessarily did so, while the origins of the modern definition of the nation in cultural, ethnic and linguistic terms were being forged elsewhere.

Rousseau restated the Contract theory in the 1760s in such a way as not only to deny that it justified the powers of the state, but also to jettison the argument that it justified the constitutional rights of the people against the state in favour of the claim that, as against the sovereign people, the state had no rights. In advancing this claim he gave a new dimension not only to democracy, but also to the concept of the political nation. As only that political community could truly be a nation in which the power lay with the whole body of the citizens, and in which the state was but their agent, the satisfaction of the national political loyalty came to require attachment not merely to a political nation but to a political nation that had been re-structured on these lines. And yet, if only because of the priority he gave to the democratic programme of merging society and the state in a higher organisation resting on the general will, Rousseau's view of what created and constituted the political nation was the same as Locke's, in that it gave priority to state rather than cultural criteria.

It is true that, in consequence of the stress he placed on the social implications of the Contract theory, he insisted, against the previous trend, that each political nation possessed its own distinctive character and that this found expression in social and cultural directions as well as in political institutions—in customs, habits, laws, and ways of life as well as in constitutions and forms of government. Most of the writers of the European Enlightenment, aware that this was increasingly coming to be the case, had deplored it as running counter to their advocacy of cosmopolitan cultural values.[1] Rousseau emphasised it. But if he felt that "the first rule that we have to follow is the national character; each people has, or ought to have, its own character", he was quick to add that "if this is lacking, it is necessary to begin by creating it".[2] It was not the national character which shaped constitutions and forms of government, indeed. "It is the institutions of the nation which form the genius, the tastes and the culture of a people . . ."[3]—above all, the institutions which reflected the relations between the citizens and the state. "The *patrie* rests on the relations of the state with its members; when these change or are destroyed, the *patrie* disappears."[4]

At the time of the revolutions in America and France, then, it was still the prevailing belief in those countries, even among men steeped in Rousseau's ideas, that, in the words of Sieyes, a nation was "a body of associates living under one common law and represented by the same legislature".[5] And the revolutions themselves did not result in any revision of this definition. In their

[1] Kemilainen, A. (Yvaskyla, 1964), *Nationalism, Problems Concerning the Word, the Concept and Classification.*
[2] Vaughan, C. E. (ed.), *Political Writings of Rousseau* (1915), Vol. II, *Projet Corse,* p. 319.
[3] ibid., Vol. II, *Considérations sur le Gouvernement de Pologne,* p. 431.
[4] Quoted in Cobban, A. (1964), *Rousseau and the Modern State* from *Rousseau's Correspondence Générale,* ed. T. Dufour, Vol. X, pp. 337–8.
[5] Quoted in Cobban, A. (1969), *The Nation State and National Self-Determination,* pp. 33—4.

pursuit of the democratic programme which Rousseau had grafted on to the idea and the function of the nation, they evolved a nationalism that was more widespread and more intense than any earlier manifestation of it. But they laid no stress on the social or cultural criteria of the nation.

As a result of the American Revolution, George III's American subjects became American citizens. But not only was there no ethnic, cultural or linguistic division between them and the society from which they broke away, as opposed to the institutional, territorial and political divergencies which increasingly separated them from it. The newly-independent American body-politic was, further, a union of states in which physical residence and political allegiance remained the only conceivable tests of citizenship, for the union as for the individual states, and in which the only actual ground for exclusion from citizenship, and that only in some of the states, was the legal condition of slavery. In 1789, again, the *roi de France et de Navarre* became the *roi des Français*. But this change, symbolising the democratic wish to join the state and the nation in a closer association, implied no departure from the established territorial conception of the nation itself towards a cultural or linguistic definition of it. Nor can any such departure be deduced from the fact that in 1791–2 the French Assembly conducted plebiscites before accepting the incorporation of Avignon and the Venaissin and of Savoy and Nice into France.

Arising as it did from the democratic conviction that the agreement of outlying communities, clearly expressed, must precede and sanction their incorporation in the French nation, the decision to hold plebiscites perhaps logically implied that other communities could opt out of the nation if they resorted to the same democratic procedure. But it did not imply a new conception of the nation, and least of all any cultural or linguistic conception of it. When the French Convention followed up the plebiscites by decreeing, at the end of 1792, the death penalty for any who attempted to destroy the unity of the new French Republic, or to detach any part of it, it was correcting, in the interests of maintaining the French as "une nation une et indivisible", the

Revolution's earlier excess of democratic fervour. It was not terminating a period in which, however briefly, the Revolution had adopted the view that membership of the French nation was something to be settled by reference to ethnic character or culture or language.

But if this view of what constitutes a nation remained alien to the French and the Americans, it was nevertheless at this very time that the social, cultural and linguistic concept of the nation was first formulated in some other European societies. From the middle of the eighteenth century, and particularly after 1770, it inspired the first Norwegian national hymn, the first Finnish national poem, a history of Norway based on the demand for Norwegian independence, the revival of the name *Belges* for the inhabitants of the Austrian Netherlands, the beginning of the Irish programme for parliamentary independence from the United Kingdom and, in Germany, the writings of Herder, the earliest and perhaps the most influential of all the theorists who have insisted that a nation rests on cultural, ethnic and linguistic uniformity and distinctiveness, and can be defined only in cultural, ethnic and linguistic terms. And we have but to list these early expressions of this theory to recognise the circumstances, so different from those obtaining in western Europe and North America, that were giving rise to it.

In most of western Europe and the United States the greater rapidity of social and economic change and the resulting intellectual ferment were producing the demand for the democratisation of the state. Except among the Catalans, the Basques, the Irish and other fringe populations, they were not producing any disaffection with the territorial and institutional conception of the nation which the centralising work of the state had succeeded in establishing. That work had a long history behind it. It was by now too advanced, and the state's assimilation of various cultural communities into tolerably homogeneous societies was too complete, for such disaffection to be widespread. In Scandinavia, the Netherlands and the German area, on the other hand, less ancient or less effective states either ruled over various cultural communities, which they had scarcely begun to assimilate into integrated societies, or else, as in Germany, divided the area of a single cultural and linguistic mass between a large number of territorial and juristic sovereignties. At the same time, social, economic and intellectual development, though it was less advanced and less rapid than in western Europe, was at last sufficient to create discontent with local, pre-national groups and loyalties.

In this situation the discontent was directed not only against the inadequacy of those groups and loyalties but also against the efforts of the existing state to replace them with a wider political loyalty to itself. Its objective was not to accelerate the growth of that wider loyalty by demanding the democratisation of the existing state and its closer association with society. It was the rejection of the existing state in favour of a movement which demanded recognition and independence for the society as a nation. And in this situation, as was later to be the case in similar circumstances throughout eastern and south-eastern Europe, and also among Belgians, Irish, Basques and other peripheral groups within the older state-nations of western Europe, the basis for this claim was the modern form of the social and cultural definition of the nation.

What distinguished this definition of the nation was not the belief that nations were the groups into which men were naturally divided, with its corollary that each nation was marked off from the others by its social and cultural characteristics. This belief had contributed the social and cultural ingredients that had been prominent in the earliest conception of the political nation in the fifteenth and sixteenth centuries. During the eighteenth century not only Rousseau, but also conservative writers like Bolingbroke and Burke, had revived it in their opposition to the increasing tendency to think of the nation as consisting only of the territories and the institutions that were held together by the power and authority of a state. But they had thought of the distinctive characteristics of the nation as being the product of history, the outcome of the influence of shared institutions, and as being natural in that sense, and it was on this point that the new definition, developed in the circumstances which obtained outside western Europe, broke new ground.

For Herder and his successors the nation was prior to history, not the product of it. It formed common institutions, as it formed common history, language, customs or religion, rather than arising from them. It was natural in the sense that these distinguishing characteristics, which gave it unity and also — because they marked it off from other nations — uniqueness, were "objective", pre-ordained. If they went unnoticed it was because they were latent or suppressed. But they were objectively ascertainable, and, if not perhaps for Herder himself,[1] then for activists wherever his doctrine applied, the goal of political activity was to develop them until the nation had been brought into the full existence which it acquired only when its uniqueness was enshrined in its own nation-based state.

As the new way of defining the nation originated separately from the movement towards democratisation — in northern rather than western Europe; in the writings of Herder and Fichte rather than those of Locke or Rousseau; with the beginnings of the Romantic revival in European thought, rather than with the great political revolutions — so it was never to acquire any but a coincidental association with it.

Not long after it was formulated, when the initial democratic idealism of the French Revolution had been diverted into imperialist expansion, it temporarily forged a close alliance with democratic forces in national resistance movements which sprang up to oppose the armies and the puppet governments of the French Republic and the Napoleonic Empire. But in the next hundred years it was repeatedly demonstrated that there was no more connection between the spread of the cultural concept of the nation and the advance of political democracy than there was between the territorial conception of the nation and authoritarianism. Established regimes, whether in Gladstone's England or in the Russia of the Tsars, adhered to the latter conception

---

[1] For Herder, who was more interested in developing the self-consciousness of the Volk than in applying his views to political nationalism, and whose ideal in the field of political ideas was a decentralised popular collectivism similar to Rousseau's, see Clark, R. T. (Berkeley, 1955), *Herder, His Life and Thought*, and Smith, A. D. (London, 1971), *Theories of Nationalism*, and Berlin, I. (Baltimore, 1965), "Herder and the Enlightenment" in Wasserman, E. A. (ed.), *Aspects of the 18th Century*.

regardless of their political hue. Movements for national independence embraced the former, whether they were led by traditional aristocracies which had survived the loss of independence by historical nations, as with the Poles or the Hungarians, or, as among cultural groups which like the Czechs or the southern Slavs had never yet existed as independent nations and possessed no native aristocracies, by populist and peasant agitators. Throughout the nineteenth century, moreover, the advocates of the cultural and ethnic version of nationalism were at odds not only with the ideology of established governments but also, and increasingly, with that of those who sought to push governments further in the democratic direction.

Historians of the first half of the nineteenth century are unable to avoid conjuring with the labels Romanticism, Liberalism and Nationalism. They frequently forget that, of these merely semantically similar words, Romanticism relates to the spirit of the age, Liberalism (like Conservatism or Socialism) denotes a political programme, and Nationalism could spell support for either the territorial or the cultural concept of the nation. If this is remembered, it will be seen that, while all articulate men were Romantics, and all in some sense Nationalist, there was almost an inverse relationship between Liberalism, properly defined as one in the range of political programmes, and attachment to the definition of the political nation in cultural, linguistic or ethnic terms. Liberals like Cavour increasingly became in this second sense the least Nationalist force, and the most Nationalist were Conservatives like Garibaldi, Socialists like Mazzini, and men who, like Napoleon III, were both Conservative and Socialist. What was true of the movement for Italian unification was true throughout Europe. And it was true also of British spectators of the European national movements of the time. Of these the least sympathetic to the cultural nationalist cause were the most radical among the Liberals—men like Cobden.[1]

---

[1] A characteristic expression of their views was Cobden's complaint in 1855 that most writers on the national problems of the Continent "take either the line of our old aristocratic diplomacy, or the modern and equally unsound and mischievous line adopted by our so-called 'democrats', in behalf of Mazzini and the 'nationalities' . . ." (Cobden to Bright, 11 Feb. 1855; B.M. Add. MS. 43650, fol. 95).

4

From the middle years of the century there was among British
and European Liberals an increase of humanitarian sympathy
with the wider cause of peoples struggling under oppressive
governments, notably those of the Sultan and the Tsar. This was
a cause which, like the growing identification of the British Liberal
Party with the Celtic cultural fringes of the United Kingdom,
conveniently combined support for the demands of cultural
nationalism with attachment to the principles of the Liberal
political programme so long as it was felt that those demands
could be satisfied by constitutional concessions to minority
nationalities, on the lines of "Home Rule". But whenever a cultural national movement demanded more, and threatened to get
out of hand, the conflict with Liberal and especially with radical-
Liberal democratic principles reappeared, to create confusion in
Liberal ranks and prevent any close alignment between Liberalism
and the cultural nationalist programme.[1] Up to the First World
War most of the foreign (and especially of the British) sympathisers
with cultural national movements continued to be romantic
Conservatives, just as most of the leaders of those movements
continued to be romantic Conservatives or romantic Socialists.

At the end of the First World War the principle that each cultural nation had the right to constitute an independent state and
to decide upon its form—a principle which now acquired the
name of national self-determination—was adopted by the Allied
and Associated Governments as their programme for the resettlement of eastern and south-eastern Europe; and their propaganda
for it emphasised its essentially liberal or democratic character.
But the propaganda was motivated by the desperate search for
total victory over the Central Powers rather than by any conviction that national self-determination would produce liberal

---

[1] It is perhaps worth emphasising that, in contrast, the liberal attachment to the
institutional and territorial concept of the nation remained close. When a nationalist
movement was based on this concept, and was thus also or even primarily a constitutional or revolutionary movement seeking the reform and liberalisation of the
existing state, as were the Persian revolutionary experiment from the early years of the
twentieth century, the Young Turk Revolution from 1908 and the Chinese nationalist
movement from 1911, most Liberals could unite in enthusiastic support for it, even if it
involved the propping-up of a multi-national state. The same was true of their sympathy for Russian radicals and for the constitutional-nationalism that was emerging
in Egypt and India.

regimes, and only Conservatives and Wilsonian Liberals accepted its argument that democracy and cultural nationalism were virtually synonymous. The propaganda and the attempt to base the peace treaty and the League of Nations on the principle of national self-determination were rejected by Socialists and by radical Liberals, who were increasingly moving towards Socialism.

For it must not be overlooked that, since the middle of the nineteenth century, the waning of Liberal distrust for the cultural concept of the nation had been more than offset by another development. Since that time, following the final defeat in western Europe of utopian or romantic Socialism by Marxist or scientific Socialism, the Socialist movement had replaced Liberalism there as the political programme which, being the most extreme in the cause of democratisation, was the political programme that was least attached to cultural nationalism — that, more than this, was so hostile to cultural nationalism that it came to advocate, or at least to tolerate, the view that the working class should give its political loyalty to the state-nation and accept the state's territorial and institutional criteria for the nation.

Building on the recognition that the nation was the natural human grouping in Rousseau's sense — in the sense that, though they were the product of common history, effort and institutions within a territory, the cultural characteristics of each nation nevertheless gave it unity and distinguished it from other nations — but adding to it Hegel's rejection of the doctrine that the cultural criteria of each nation were objectively ascertainable — his insistence that what defined and fulfilled a people was, on the contrary, its submission to its own state — Marx and Engels deplored the idea that every cultural group, particularly the economically undeveloped group, must evolve into a political nation, and favoured the large, historical, state-made political nations that already existed and that were multi-national in their cultural composition. "All changes", wrote Engels in 1859, "if they are to last, must start from the effort to give the large but viable European nations more and more their true national boundaries, which are determined by language and sympathy, while the ruins of peoples, which are still found here and there and which are no longer capable of a national existence, are absorbed by the larger nations and either become a part of them or maintain themselves as ethnographic monuments without political significance."[1] And thereafter most socialists adopted this position—it was that of the Fabians and George Bernard Shaw as well as of Rosa Luxemburg —and squared it with their objection to emphasising nationalism in any of its forms, as being the tool of the bourgeoisie, by using Engels's justification for it. To create political nations out of small under-developed peoples would be to set up a barrier to economic progress. The great state-nations could alone be the vehicle for industrial capitalist advance and thus for the development of class-conscious industrial proletariats.

The fact that the new cultural concept of the political nation was not necessarily democratic, liberal or socialist in its implications, and was indeed unwelcome to liberals and socialists, did not impede its progress. Once formulated, it was appealed to whenever the combination of social, economic and political conditions became similar to that which had first produced it. As the relation between states and cultural groupings was widely at variance with its claims, political discontent mobilised under its banner wherever economic and social development was on the one hand sufficient to produce discontent with existing political forms but was, on the other hand, insufficiently advanced or insufficiently rapid to permit the state to make progress with the assimilation of its various peoples. As this situation came to prevail from the beginning of the nineteenth century at different times in different areas, first in Europe and then beyond, liberalism and socialism have since then suffered repeated and lasting defeats at its hands.

In the same situation, again, its advance has everywhere put on the defensive not only existing states, but also the territorial or state criteria of the nation. It is not the relationship of nationalism with democracy, indeed, but this conflict between two definitions of the political nation, continually renewed, which provides the clue to the development of modern nationalism. In the case of this

[1] Quoted in Smith, A. D. (1971), *Theories of Nationalism*, p. 73, from Engels, F., *Po und Rhein*.

conflict, however, the one sure guide through its confusing ramifications will be found to lie in one simple fact. While initially it almost everywhere exerted a far more powerful emotive appeal, the objective cultural definition of the nation has everywhere yielded to the definition of the nation in accordance with the criteria of territory, historical development, common institutions and the state.

The explanation of this process consists in part of a logical point. The belief that the territory of each state should coincide with a culturally and linguistically uniform area may be implemented equally well in two different ways. It would be fulfilled if each existing cultural and linguistic area were to acquire its own state. But it would also be fulfilled if each existing state were to complete the cultural and linguistic assimilation of its inhabitants. In historical fact, moreover, the first of these programmes, if able to make progress at all, was absorbed into the second because it was advanced at a time when, by extending political participation to the broadest masses and increasing the functions which the state performed for society, social and economic development was slowly forcing or enabling the state to accelerate its assimilating efforts.

In the course of doing so, it gave greater emphasis to such social and cultural susceptibilities as were not incompatible with the state conception of the nation. This conception, whose relevance had hitherto been restricted to limited sectors of the population and whose concern had hitherto been narrowly political, could thus widen its appeal by satisfying some of the aspirations which were met by the cultural conception of the nation. But its rival lacked this flexibility, and this was a further reason for the temporary nature of its victories. It had its greatest success, as the state conception of the nation had the greatest difficulty in making its impact, where cultural groups had been least assimilated and cultural divisions were at their widest. It was in just these conditions, however, that it proved to be least practicable as a principle on which existing political communities could be reconstructed or new political communities created—and that it was accordingly abandoned with the least delay in favour of the state conception of the nation.

Among the most fully-assimilated populations the cultural conception could scarcely even take root. Here, it is true, states ruled over more than one cultural group. But the assimilation of the groups either had proceeded over centuries, as in western Europe and in Japan,[1] or else, as in the United States, was the inescapable counterpart of the inflow of immigrant populations. Accordingly, the prevailing concept of the nation continued to be the territorial and institutional concept which had everywhere prevailed till the eighteenth century. By the *Académie Française* in 1878 the nation was still defined as it had been by Sieyes in 1789: "the totality of persons born or naturalized in the country and living under a single government". In all these societies this continued to be the orthodox definition. And wherever, as was only exceptionally the case, the rival concept of the nation raised its head, in Ireland, among the Flemish element in Belgium or among the Southerners in their struggle with the North in the United States, it was on this basis and with wide public support that it was suppressed by force.

In central Europe the outcome was eventually the same. Everywhere else in Europe one state ruled more than one community. In the German area, as also in the Italian, numerous states ruled a single area which appeared to be culturally and linguistically uniform. Here, as we have seen, from the moment of their revival, the cultural and linguistic criteria of the nation not unnaturally had a strong appeal. And here, if only when harnessed to the interests of the strongest of the states, they made a powerful contribution to the creation of new unified nations in the middle years of the nineteenth century. As unification pro-

---

[1] Development in Japan was not dissimilar to that of the western state-nations, though it took place later and was complicated by their earlier advance. In the last days of the Shogunate its supporters and its opponents vied with each other in stressing the cultural criteria of the nation against the increasing incursions of the western foreigner. For some time past, however, the Shogunate had emphasised the state conception of the nation in its effort to centralise and reduce the feudal nobility, after the fashion of the European centralising monarchies in the seventeenth and eighteenth centuries. And the movement which produced the overthrow of the Shogunate and the restoration of the Meiji emperor, in 1868, was not unlike that which led to the French Revolution. Though it was assisted by feudal reaction to the Shogunate, its basic object was the more radical rejection of feudal forms and traditional attitudes and their replacement by a more modern regulatory state, with closer links with society and more enthusiastic acceptance of western ideas. Its success was thus followed by even greater emphasis on the criteria of the nation that were associated with the state.

ceeded, however, and as Prussia and Piedmont turned these areas into areas that were ruled by a single state but that turned out to be less culturally uniform than theorists had supposed, national feeling changed its character. In the more articulate sections of the population the earlier attachment to the cultural nation gave way to loyalty to the new territorial nation, and to its state, its institutions, its flag and its armed forces. Nor was this all. In Italy the achievement of territorial unification was quickly followed by a programme of political unification which imposed centralisation or Piedmontisation on resistant regional cultural divisions. In the new German Reich, as *Kleindeutsch* sentiment replaced *Grossdeutsch* sentiment, so did the belief that his state must decide the individual's nationality replace the belief that his nationality must appoint his state, and the result was even more forcible denationalisation of minorities—of Poles and Danes—than was being adopted further west.

Further east, the Magyars led the way in the same direction. Before obtaining the compromise of autonomy for Hungary within the Austro-Hungarian empire in 1867, they had exploited in their struggle against Vienna both the territorial concept of the nation, which had been bequeathed to them by the long earlier history of Hungary as an independent kingdom, and the cultural concept of it, which was fuelled by their continuing cohesion as Magyars. The resulting confusion of thought and terminology with reference to the nation was enshrined in a new Hungarian law of nationalities in 1868. "All citizens of Hungary form a single nation—the indivisible unitary Magyar nation—to which all citizens of the country belong irrespective of nationality."[1] But if both of the definitions of the nation were thus amalgamated in this legislation, there was no ambiguity about the programme which, so soon after Hungary had secured its autonomy, it unleashed. It was the programme of safeguarding and strengthening Hungary's territorial and institutional autonomy by bringing about the compulsory assimilation of Hungary's cultural minorities on the basis of the state conception of the nation.

---

[1] For the translation, which is as precise as it can be in the circumstances, see Macartney, C. A. (1934), *National States and National Minorities*, p. 119.

Elsewhere the conflict between the two concepts of the nation was more delayed and more complicated, and the outcome more protracted. In western Europe communications, economic change and social mobility had been advanced by the centralising, levelling state, and had at the same time been modifying the patrimonial, dynastic and imperial attitudes of the state, ever since the end of the Middle Ages. In Europe's northern and central areas the same processes had been at work since the beginning of the eighteenth century. Further east they made little impact before the middle of the nineteenth century. Until then the Habsburg, Romanov and Ottoman structures which ruled throughout eastern and south-eastern Europe remained multi-cultural or poly-ethnic empires, rather than becoming multi-national states, despite the imitative and premature modernising efforts of their "enlightened despots" since the eighteenth century. Beyond Europe, in Asia, Africa and elsewhere, this was also the character of the empires that were just beginning to be established or extended by the European Powers. And in these areas, as well as beginning later, the development of nationalism was complicated by another consideration.

In Germany, Italy and Scandinavia, as in Hungary, the cultural groups were tolerably homogeneous and geographically well-defined when they reached the point at which the political loyalty began to transfer itself from the family, the neighbourhood, the province and the religious community to a wider political framework. Whether it was ruled by a single alien state, as was that of the Norwegians, the Finns or the Magyars, or was split up under several separate sovereignties, as in Germany and Italy, the cultural group's response was regulated by this fact. In its resistance to the centralising effort of the existing state, which was now becoming effective for the first time, it conceived of itself as a nation, and turned first to the cultural conception of the political nation as the basis of the demand for its own state or for a different state, even if this conception of the nation yielded to the state conception of the nation if and when the new state was acquired. Elsewhere, however, cultural homogeneity and geographical frame were both so lacking when this point was reached that no such simple outcome could result.

Throughout eastern and south-eastern Europe cultural divisions remained very large in some respects, as a result of the economic and social backwardness of the societies and the political backwardness of the states. As a result of such social and political development as had taken place, on the other hand, the cultural groups shared some social similarities, so that between the outside extremes the differences between them were graded and muted, and they were, moreover, geographically inextricably mixed. On top of this, though the Magyars and the Muscovites were exceptions here, state frontiers of considerable antiquity cut across such areas as remained homogeneous by language or other cultural tests. In these conditions the political loyalty could not focus uniformly or steadily on either conception of the nation. When, as was increasingly the case after the middle years of the nineteenth century, it outgrew the older forms, more local or more extensive, of clan or religion, and sought to centre on the nation, the situation was one in which from individual to individual it split, and in which according to circumstances it oscillated, between attachment to the principle that the cultural group, conceived of as a nation, should have its own state, and attachment to the existing state.

If nationalism took the form of loyalty to the state, it fluctuated yet again, between loyalty to the antique structure of the Tsars, the Habsburgs and the Sultans and, on the other hand, to the programme of political revolutionaries who, on the model of the French Revolution, sought not to overthrow the state, but to replace the dynasties with states that were more representative of society and more capable of modernising it. In either case, however, the loyalty was loyalty to a state that remained at the imperial stage. For in these conditions the state was bound to continue the assimilation of its inhabitants and the consolidation of its society, work which in this area was far short of completion. The revolutionary officers who overthrew the Obrenovitch dynasty in Serbia in 1904 were still more intent than it had been on pursuing its "Greater Serbia" ambitions. After the Young Turks had overthrown the Sultan in 1908 their Turkification policy outdid in intensity the programme of Islamisation by which he had hoped to Ottomanise and centralise his lands. In Russia, in the same way, the socialist and "westernising" revolutionary movement had no quarrel with the effort of the Tsar's government to bring about the Russification of Finland, Russian Poland, the Ukraine, and Russia's other western provinces.

Instead of either supporting the centralising policies of the existing state or seeking to accelerate them by revolution, the national loyalty might attach itself to the cultural group. In that case the problem was how and where the loyalty could come to rest when wider and narrower definitions of the cultural nation overlapped in conditions of ethnical confusion. And the outcome was the distortion of nationalism. For two extreme ideologies resulted from emphasising cultural criteria as the basis of a political nation in these conditions. The first was the pan-ism which appeared in a variety of forms — pan-Slavism, pan-Islamism, pan-Germanism, pan-Turanianism. The other was the traditionalism which, in its fanatical defence of cultural purity against either the encroachment of the state or the assertion of wider cultural criteria, redirected the political loyalty back to the smallest and strictest of cultural divisions — to the province, the tribe and the clan.

When so much conflict prevailed between and within alternative nationalist programmes and ideologies — between subjectivist state nationalism and objectivist cultural nationalism; between support for the centralising and levelling policies of integrationist imperial governments and the wish to overthrow those governments in favour of modernisation and integration by revolutionary state regimes; between the pan-ism and the tribalism which accompanied the effort to define the nation in cultural terms — two consequences were bound to follow. The conflict kept nationalist and other forms of group self-consciousness alive, and even created it in the first place, when social and economic advance was not in itself sufficient to do so. On the other hand, it so stultified all programmes for national integration or national secession that, far from settling the fate of this vast area, the development of nationalism in the area was largely determined by the play of force and the course of events. But one general conclusion may be extracted from the confusion.

More vividly than ever before, the extension of nationalism to eastern and south-eastern Europe illustrated the impracticability of the cultural definition of the nation — its inability to provide a basis for the construction of a political nation — in just those circumstances in which it exerted its greatest appeal. Whenever it was made the justification for establishing new states and the guide in fixing their frontiers, as it increasingly was from the 1870s, when the retreat of the Turkish empire from Europe was accelerated, to the collapse of all the empires at the end of the First World War, it had to compromise from the outset with other justifications and with intractable obstacles. Yugoslavism, a compromise between the extremes of pan-slavism and provincialism and also between cultural nationalism and the state-nationalism of Greater Serbia, was one of the characteristic results. Whenever a new state was brought into existence, its cultural national justification, compromised from the outset, was further diluted by the determination and the need to justify on other grounds — possession, history, geography, defence — the claim to whatever territory the state could seize and the assimilation of the cultural minorities it inevitably acquired.

That the cultural and ethnical conditions of eastern and south-eastern Europe were incompatible with the demands of cultural nationalism was finally confirmed after 1919 by the failure of the attempt to base the post-war resettlement of the area on the principle of national self-determination. But if the attempt to define the political nation exclusively in cultural terms again gave way to the need to have regard to criteria associated with the state, it now made the struggle between the two ideas of the nation in this area more bitter and protracted than it had ever been. And in this struggle the state criteria of the nation were themselves pushed to extreme lengths.

These criteria — and the nationalist or nationalising programmes of those who embrace them — require the assimilation of the state's population. If force is necessary for that purpose, they justify the use of force. Until the nineteenth century they were asserted against loyalties which, though they competed with loyalty to the state's conception of the nation, were the wider loyalties to a church or the narrower loyalties to a locality or an interest; and usually, if necessary by force, the state prevailed. But when the state's conception of the nation was confronted by a different conception of the nation, resistance to assimilation was increased, and so was the use of force to achieve assimilation. On the other hand force now had the effect of redoubling the resistance and of encouraging the growth of cultural nationalism.

Nowhere was this dilemma so acute as in eastern and south-eastern Europe where, after 1870 especially, social and political developments simultaneously produced both the rise of cultural nationalism and the adoption of centralising policies by states which, being either contented or constrained to rule multi-cultural empires, had previously not forced the pace of assimilation within their territories or had failed in the attempt to do so. It was here, therefore, in a new context, that centralisation by the state first took on a new emphasis. Hitherto, it had sought the absorption of minority groups into an all-embracing cultural and political nation. Now, the attempt to create a unified nation involved the suppression of all divergences from the cultural pattern of the dominant group, no less than from its political system. The aim of nationalising the state's population gave way to that of denationalising the minorities in it.

From this aim, which had inspired the Magyar nationality laws and which thereafter underlay the emphasis on the denationalisation of minorities in the Russification and Turkification programmes, it was but a short step to the position in which the state, instead of being opposed to the cultural definition of the nation, took it over and turned it to the state's own use. When that definition claimed that each cultural nation should have its own state, the defence against it easily became the claim that it was the task of the state to defend the territory of the cultural nation by depressing or expelling the populations which it could not assimilate, and even to extend it. With the collapse of the 1919 settlement of eastern and south-eastern Europe this step was taken. The final outcome, with its emphasis on expansion, was National-Socialism.

Other elements besides nationalism and imperialism went into the making of this ideology. But its version of nationalism and imperialism, or its relationship to nationalism and imperialism, was one of its distinctive features. In other directions, at a time when conflict between revolutionary and reactionary radicalism had driven them to extremes, it fused them to produce a political philosophy of which the beginning and the end was the nihilistic worship of force. In the same way, as a result of the impossibility of reconciling their claims in the extreme forms which they acquired in eastern and south-eastern Europe after 1919, it fused the cultural with the state criteria of the nation so as to produce a racialist justification of conquest.

Its starting-point was the state definition of the nation in that form of it which Hegel had developed in answer to the "objective" cultural definition of the nation. "The higher personality is a nation only in so far as it is a state. The nation does not exist to generate the state . . . the nation is created by the state."[1] As thus reiterated in the Fascist doctrine which was its totalitarian prototype, this remained the central tenet of Nazism. But as well as insisting that the state, not the nation, was the sole repository of the political loyalty, Nazism repaid the nation for its submission to the state by conferring on the state the task of preserving the cultural purity of the nation in accordance with a definition of the nation that, in its emphasis on the criterion of race and the doctrine of the survival of the fittest race, was more exclusive and more "objective" than any previous cultural definition. And armed with this powerful combination of the state/nation with a biological test of membership of the nation, by which non-members were automatically excluded, it embarked on expansion of which the aim was not traditional imperialism, not the rule of the state over more than one cultural community nor the assimilation of different cultural groups, but the conquest of territory and the subjection or the elimination of other peoples by a master race.

Of the other elements that went to produce the extreme of National-Socialism not the least influential was the success of the

---

[1] Quoted in Barker, E. (1942), *Reflections on Government*, p. 26, from *La Dottrina da Fascismo*.

Bolsheviks in seizing and retaining the power of the state in Russia
from 1917. As well as driving millions to embrace Nazi doctrines,
from fear that Bolshevism would spread, this directly shaped their
formulation. Their fusion of the cultural with the state criteria of
the nation itself led, perhaps inescapably, to the distortion of
nationalism by the emphasis on race. But that emphasis was also
a desperate attempt to counter the distortion of the Communist
appeal to class that resulted from Bolshevism's compromise with
nationalism. For despite its starting-point in the dismissal of
national in preference to class loyalty—to proletarian internationalism—Communism in power, like Bolshevism, was driven
to come to terms with nationalism.

Within Russia itself, where it inherited the government of a
poly-ethnic or multi-national empire, it easily accommodated
itself to the preference of its prophets for the state or historical
conception of the nation. Such concessions as it made to the claims
and susceptibilities of Russia's various cultural nationalities were
always subjected to the centralising, modernising and assimilating
programme of the state. As an international doctrine it was less
able to follow what its prophets had laid down. For them the large,
historical, multi-national political structure, ruled by the centralising state and based on the state conception of the political
nation, had been tolerated, indeed supported against the threat
of cultural nationalism, because it would favour the expansion of
proletariats which was the prerequisite of the victory of proletarian
internationalism over nationalism of any kind. For Communism
this argument had necessarily to be reversed. In power in a backward and a weakened society, and one that was isolated in a world
of alien capitalist societies, it called on the socialists of the world
to unite behind the belief that proletarian internationalism was
essential if Russia's national interests were to be safeguarded and
advanced.

By thus harnessing socialism to nationalism, Communism
evolved into the most universalist pan-ism of all time—the pan-
ism of those who, far from hoping to found a nation on criteria of
national cultural affinity that were too wide to be politically
practicable, gave their political loyalty to the state which was

associated with a single blue-print for regenerating and standardising every society. By contrast, and by way of retaliation, the National-Socialist doctrine, harnessing nationalism to race, was the ultimate stage of the process foreshadowed by the extremism of national self-determination — the process by which loyalty to the nation would be replaced by submission to tribal barbarism.

But if these responses to the stress of European conditions in the inter-war years involved the transfer of the political loyalty from the nation to the empire or the tribe, or to both, subsequent developments in Europe, and now also beyond Europe, were soon to show that this transfer was only temporary. In closing this account of the evolution of nationalism we do not conclude the history of nationalism, but only an analysis of the narrow limits within which it operated up to the Second World War. It is within these same limits that it has had to operate since, and that it must and will continue to work. They are the limits set by the bases of nationalism. If these make it sure that nationalism will continue, they also make it sure that by 1945, except in one direction, the limits had been thoroughly explored.

What had not yet been established was whether nationalism, so clearly different from other expressions of the political loyalty and yet so closely allied to them, is incompatible, as are tribalism or imperialism, with internationalism. Before we glance at the operation of nationalism in its latest phase we must now turn to the history of the modern international system and see what light it throws upon this as yet unsettled question.

PART II:
THE INTERNATIONAL SYSTEM

CHAPTER FIVE

The Rise of the Modern International System

International systems, systems of relations between states, may be traced back to the beginning of recorded time, even if this is far from being true of what we now understand by the nation and the state. The earliest extant treaty comes down to us, it seems, from *circa* 2500 B.C. At one level, in its technical devices, the modern system has not been much more sophisticated than its predecessors.

A treaty of 1278 B.C. between the Pharaoh and the Hittites incorporates practically every stipulation that a treaty might contain today. Move on to the ancient Greeks and it at once emerges that they were no less familiar than we are with virtually the entire range of diplomatic resources—with leagues and alliances, with arbitration, with non-aggression pacts, with the balance of power. Or perhaps we should say that we are scarcely more advanced. When we compare ourselves with men in Europe in the seventeenth and eighteenth centuries we cannot in all matters even say this. It is impossible not to admire the meticulous care with which they arranged their alliances and built their balances—the calculation, even, with which they began and ended their wars. They wielded in these directions an expertise to which we no longer attain—to which, indeed, we no longer aspire. For if there has been a falling-off from their technical standards since their time, a general decline relieved only by the Bismarckian talent of occasional and unusual men, this has been due not so much to a movement towards mediocrity among statesmen as to a fundamental shift of aims and assumptions in the conduct of international relations.

The modern international system was the product of this shift. In its technical devices it has registered little advance, if any, beyond its predecessors. In the expertise with which it has used these devices there has even been some decline. But it has differed in its operation from all earlier systems because it has rested on, and been associated with, the only significant change that has so far occurred in history in the central ideas which men have brought to the conduct of relations between states.

This change took place during the eighteenth century. Ever since the fifteenth century, at least in Europe, international communications had been expanding and quickening; the book and the press had been sharpening men's minds and undermining maxims; bureaucracy had been finding its feet. The natural consequence of these developments had been a steady movement from the same time towards more continuous diplomacy in a diplomatic system that was more articulated than any earlier one. Not until the eighteenth century, however, even in Europe, was this movement followed by any basic reshaping of the assumptions and presuppositions which men had brought to bear on international relations for centuries. And not until our own day did the new outlook which then began to prevail show signs of yielding before another shift of ideas of the magnitude of that which set in two hundred years ago.

Of all the indications of this change, the earliest was the decay in Europe, indeed the rejection there, of a long-established approach to the issue of war and peace.

In all international systems, and not only in the modern one, there have been men who have urged the desirability or the necessity of permanent peace. In early modern Europe, and particularly from the outbreak of the Thirty Years' War in the early years of the seventeenth century, such men became more numerous, their plans more prolific and more precise, than in any earlier time or place in history. It is scarcely surprising that they have since been widely regarded as the originators of the modern peace-movement of the past hundred years. But if we look closely at their proposals—at their drafts for diets, congresses, unions, federations and leagues—we are brought up sharp by a remarkable fact. With scarcely an exception, they had repeated basic ideas which had undergone by the early years of the eighteenth century no fundamental change from those which had been common to the aspirations of the papacy during the twelfth century and the propaganda of the papacy's critics at the end of the thirteenth century, the days of Dante, of which we shall say more later on. They had not been peace-plans, indeed, in the modern sense of that term.

Their purpose had not been to establish peace between separate states. It had not even been to establish peace by means of that fusion of all separate states under a single world government whose advocates have increased the variety, though not the credibility, of the modern peace-movement during the twentieth century. It had been either the reconstruction of the unified Christendom which had flourished, their authors believed, under the Pope or the Emperor in the Middle Ages or—and this more frequently with the passage of time—the erection of a new secular Empire or Republic of Europe. Within the Christendom or the Europe of their plans they held, indeed, that war would cease. But order and authority there, and sometimes also religious uniformity, were prized no less than peace; while beyond the pale, against the Muscovite, the pagan and the Turk, Europe's order, authority and uniformity would pave the way to sound defence, to glorious conquest, to more efficient war.

We should not look askance at these objectives. The states that made up Europe's international system remained in some ways primitive states, for which empire and expansion was the logical aim. The states which bordered on the system, those of the Muscovite and the Turk, were still more primitive. The pre-industrial societies within the system remained wide open to particularist or separatist threat, to trans-national religious conflicts and millenarian cults, to oppression, famine and endless other sources of civil war. It was natural that essays addressed to the system's improvement should share its preoccupations even while hoping to mend its ways. But the consistent repetition of these ideas during the previous two hundred years serves to draw attention to two developments of the middle years of the eighteenth century.

The more obvious of these developments was the demise of the ideas themselves. Jean-Jacques Rousseau, the most considerable in a long succession of their advocates, was also the last intelligent writer to toy with them. As many had done before him, he urged the establishment of a European Commonwealth in his *Extrait du Projet de Paix Perpétuelle de Monsieur L'Abbé de Saint-Pierre*, an essay written in 1756–8 and published in 1761. Unlike most of his predecessors, Rousseau included Russia in his scheme. Though he still excluded the Turks, his arguments retained none of the overtones of European crusade and defence against other civilisations, overtones which had been fading for some time. He maintained as powerfully as any earlier writer, however, that his Commonwealth would succeed in establishing peace only if it were given "a coercive force capable of compelling every state to obey its common resolves . . . and firm enough to make it impossible for any member to withdraw at his own pleasure the moment he conceives his private interest to clash with that of the whole body". But he did not maintain this for long. In another essay of 1756–8, indeed, he dismissed his own or, rather, Saint-Pierre's proposal as being "an absurd dream".

His change of front came from his realisation that the establishment, let alone the maintenance, of such a Commonwealth "demands a concurrence of wisdom in so many heads and a fortuitous concurrence of so many interests such as chance can hardly be expected to bring about" — and that "in default of such an agreement the only thing left is force . . .". But this sense of the illogicality of organising war as the means of establishing peace, which is the main burden of the second essay, his *Jugement sur la Paix Perpétuelle*, was itself the outcome of Rousseau's participation in a second, broader development which was soon to transform the character of all internationalist writings. This was the emergence between the 1730s and the 1760s of a generation of men who, shifting their gaze from the Middle Ages, except as an object of mockery or a subject for scholarship, shattered for ever — or at least until its revival in our own century—the ancient concern for the right ordering of Christendom.

They did this by advancing to the view that, far from being a fallen empire or a faded federation in need of reconstruction, Europe was a collection of independent, if interlocked, States. The result was a conception of the international system of a kind which no man before them had entertained. Not even the Italian city-statesmen of the fifteenth and sixteenth centuries had approached it. For all their novel experience of the problems of rivalry and collaboration between contiguous and closely interlocked political communities—an experience which explains their invention of the resident ambassador, or permanent embassy, the first addition to be made to the stock of diplomatic techniques handed down by the classical world—they had been debarred from doing so by either the violence of their separatism or the tenacity of their interest in Italy's imperial and papal past.

For all its shared historical development, its cultural and social uniformity, Europe was divided into separate political states. The essence of a truly international system was precisely a tension between interconnectedness on the one hand—common history, culture and social institutions—and political division and the resultant rivalries on the other. In no civilisation before their own had this tension existed. Their Europe was in this respect unique. This new conception of Europe was first developed by Montesquieu in *De l'Esprit des Lois* (1748), Voltaire in *The Age of Louis XIV* (1751), Hume in *Essays Literary, Moral and Political* (1751) and Rousseau in *Jugement sur la Paix Perpétuelle* (written by 1758 though not published till 1784).

Despite this advance, schemes for achieving peace by reorganising the empire of Europe or restoring the unity of Christendom were resuscitated during the wars that followed the French Revolution. More than that, the French then attempted, the first time ever, to put them into effect. But even before the Napoleonic empire had finally discredited these schemes by dispersing the delusion that they were schemes for obtaining and maintaining peace, they had been supplanted by their modern equivalent, as a result of a further advance in international ideas. In the 1780s, in essays that were very different in quality, men as far apart as Bentham and Kant had propounded the view that there could be no solution to the problem of war unless and until a truly international system had evolved a truly international law.

Although it was a logical development of the earlier advance to the modern conception of an international system, this conviction did not derive directly from Montesquieu, Voltaire and Hume. On the contrary, Bentham and Kant were led to it by their reaction against the first effect of the insistence of these earlier writers that Europe was a system of politically independent, if closely associated, states. This had taken two forms. For some the argument that war was inescapable between such states had softened into the complacent belief that the virtues of this system at least outdid its defects — that, as Burke and Gibbon were fond of saying, it maintained the liberty of states and limited the scale and frequency of their wars, even if it did not guarantee perpetual peace between them. For others, notably Voltaire and the *philosophes*, it had been replaced by a jaunty confidence that, given such a system, war could easily be avoided if states would listen to reason and pursue "the wise policy" of maintaining between themselves a balance of power. By one man, however, these two approaches had been combined to produce the first modern statement of international law.

Emmerick de Vattel had carved himself a permanent place in international legal history by imposing the new view of Europe as an international system upon the accumulated lumber of post-medieval legal thought. His starting-point had been just that tension between Europe's cosmopolitanism in culture and Europe's political division into separate states on which that view had focussed. For his forerunners either the cosmopolitanism had had its counterpart in an external and pre-existing natural or moral law, and this alone had been the source of international law — or else the political division had been an insuperable obstacle to, a standing denial of, the possibility of any international law at all. In his *Le Droit des Gens, ou Principes de la Loi Naturelle, appliqués à la Conduite et aux Affaires des Nations et des Souverains* (1758), as the title of the book suggests, Vattel squared the circle. For him the only possible basis for an international law was the political division into separate states; and it was the first rule of the pre-existing natural law that this should be so. But if grand results flowed from his insistence that the sovereign state, the grand outcome of natural law, was thus alone invested with the duty to develop international law for the better regulation of interstate relations, so did a great dilemma.

It enabled Vattel to perceive the quality of state-hood, the "statishness" of all states, and so to emphasise as never before the respect due from every state to the sovereign equality of every other state by virtue of its being a state in a system of states. Whereas previous legal writers had been concerned only to civilise conflict—to systematise the rules to be followed in con-ducting war and making peace—it enabled him to give equal emphasis to the need for an international law in time of peace. Based on such organising principles, the book he produced in 1758 is the first guide to international legal practice that is reasonably intelligible, even to an international lawyer, in the twentieth century. It was also, however, the first such guide to be adopted as a handbook by governments, and for a very good reason. In 1794 Charles James Fox castigated the disposition of states to throw their Vattel into the sea when its principles disagreed with their interests. He was missing the point. Because of its emphasis on the rights as well as on the duties of states, on the sovereignty of each state as well as on the sovereign equality of all, the book possessed that attraction for governments which has ever since endeared to them the international legal profession as a whole. In every controversy it could be quoted on either side. In a quarrel between states it legalised both parties by preserving the un-restricted right of every state to go to war.

Grotius, Vattel's seventeenth-century predecessor, had recog-nised this right by conceding that "by the consent of nations a rule has been introduced that all wars conducted on both sides, by authority of the sovereign power, were held to be just wars". Long before Grotius's time, this argument had shaped the theory of the just war during the later Middle Ages. But when Vattel reasserted it as a necessary rule of law, Rousseau was already suspicious of it.

> After setting down the true principles of political right [he
> wrote at the end of his *Contrat Social* (1762)] and trying to
> establish the state on the basis of those principles, I should
> complete my study by considering the foreign relations of the
> state, including the law of nations (*le droit des gens*), commerce,
> the rights of war and conquest, international law (*le droit public*),
> leagues, negotiations, treaties and so forth. But all this forms a
> new field which is too vast for my limited vision.

And twenty years later Rousseau's abortive attempt to distinguish
between Vattel's law and a true international law, between the
droit des gens and the *droit public*, became for Bentham and Kant
the point of their new departure.

Kant spoke for both when he wrote, in what he called the second
definitive article of the second section of *Perpetual Peace*, that

> Grotius, Pufendorf, Vattel and the others — miserable com-
> forters all of them — are still always quoted cordially for the
> justification of an outbreak of war, although their philosophically
> or diplomatically composed codes have not, nor could have the
> slightest legal force, since the States as such stand under no
> common legal constraint; and there is not an example of a
> State having been ever moved to desist from its purpose by
> arguments . . . armed with the testimonies of such important
> men.

On the other hand, both had concluded that this gap could be
closed only by further international legal development. Between
Rousseau's time and theirs the view that Europe was an international system had become fully established. Not only had Vattel
used it to refashion international law; his work had met with
rapid acceptance because it had matched the international system
as the system really operated. What more natural than that critics
of the system should now also criticise international law; should

point out that, being so well adjusted to the system, it was not calculated to make the system into what an international system ought to be; should concentrate, therefore, on the necessity for this purpose of improving international law? For Bentham and Kant, indeed, this was so much the right way forward that they rejected the programme for improving the international system by amalgamating states, or by imposing international political organisation upon them, that had dominated internationalist thinking up to Rousseau's day, and that was to recapture it from the end of the nineteenth century.

This has not been the standard interpretation of their outlook. Bentham is commonly treated as a pioneer of the League of Nations, with its sanctions and its collective security guarantees, Kant as an advocate of world federation. Neither of these verdicts will stand up to a close examination of their writings. The burden of Bentham's *Principles of International Law*—four essays, including his *Plan for an Universal and Perpetual Peace*, written between 1786 and 1789, but not published until 1843—was that peace depended on developing the resources of law, reason and public opinion against the machinations of governments. Of interference by government, as opposed to regulation by the rationality and the sovereignty of law, there should be as little as possible above states and between them, as within them. His sole institutional proposal was for the establishment by treaty of a common tribunal or court of arbitration, though he also called this a "Congress or Diet". It was his firm belief that, given liberty of the press, the only sanction that would be required to ensure obedience by states to the court's awards was the power of public opinion. For Kant, even more decisively than for Bentham, treaty agreement between sovereign states was the only means by which the international system might be improved.

It is this fact that has given rise to the erroneous belief that he advocated federation. The commentators have overlooked that, though in his *Idea for a Universal History* (1784) and *Thoughts on Perpetual Peace* (1795) he frequently used such expressions as the "federation of free states", "free federation", and "a federal union of nations", he derived them directly from the latin *foedus* and used them strictly to mean agreement reached and maintained by treaty. Nor did he leave any room for misinterpretation on this point. Distinguishing between these expressions and the idea of a single state of nations (*Völkerbund*), he went out of his way to emphasise that the latter was logically irrelevant as a solution to problems between states. A "state of nations contains a contradiction . . .; many nations would in a single state constitute only one nation, which is contradictory since we are here considering the rights of the nations towards each other as long as they constitute different states and are not joined together into one." He stated that a single state of nations, in the modern sense of a world federation, was never likely to be practicable. And far from accepting the continuing independence of states as merely inescapable, he insisted as forcefully as Vattel had done that it was morally right. "A state is not a possession like the soil . . . It is a society of men which no one but themselves is called on to command or dispose of. Since, like a tree, such a state has its roots, to incorporate it as a graft into another state is to take away its existence as a moral person and to make of it a thing."

What Kant propounded, then, was not federation in our sense of the term, but collaboration between states under an improved law of nations. When perfected, the law of nations would constitute a "Cosmopolitan or World Law", even a "world constitution", for the "union of nations". But this union would be one in which "every state, even the smallest, may expect its security and its right not from its own power or its own legal views, but . . . from decisions according to the united will of them all"; and this united will, far from requiring submission to an effective international executive authority, would result from the development of the law of nations to the point at which it constituted "a counter-balance to the intrinsically healthy resistance of many states against each other, in consequence of their freedom". Even when the union had been brought about, "states will not subject themselves (as men do in the state of nature) to laws and the enforcement of such laws". Although "only such a union may under existing conditions stem the tide of the law-evading bellicose propensities in men", it would thus remain "unfortunately subject to constant danger of their eruption". It would indeed be "*a union of a particular kind*".[1] And what would distinguish it was the fact that, whereas under the existing law of nations states could obtain their rights only by war, the basis of the improved international law would be a pacific treaty "which tries to end *all* wars for ever".

Bentham and Kant propounded the same novel solution for the problem of war. In one respect, however, they were poles apart. With all the optimism of the *philosophes*, Bentham believed that the solution might be implemented at once, if only men would be sensible. Kant expected it to be postponed until some day in the future when men would have been taught to be wise by their further social evolution and by much bitter experience.

"Europe . . .", wrote Bentham, "would have had no wars but for the feudal system, religious antipathy, the rage of conquest and the uncertainties of succession. Of these four causes, the first is happily extinct everywhere, the second and third almost every-where — at any rate in France and England — and the last might, if not already extinguished, be so with great ease." "Supposing Great Britain and France thoroughly agreed, the principal dif-ficulties would be removed to the establishment of a plan of general and permanent pacification for all Europe," and to the functioning of his court or Tribunal of Peace. Kant was convinced that his idea of a cosmopolitan or world law, though not "a fantastic or utopian way of looking at law, but a necessary completion of the unwritten code of constitutional and international law to make it a public law of mankind", could not be adopted until "remote parts of the world can enter into relationships which eventually become public and legal", and not merely the states of Europe. Nor would even Europe conform to it until its states were ready to adopt it as the corrective to their continuing rivalry.

At any time until then, it "would not by itself have protected [them] from violence and war", however clearly it might be formulated. It would not do this — they would not implement it — until

[1] Kant's italics.

nature has again used quarrelsomeness, in this case that of the great societies and states, as a means of discovering a condition of quiet and security through the very antagonism inevitable among them ... Wars, the excessive and never-ending preparation for wars, and the want which every state must feel even in the midst of peace—all these are means by which nature instigates attempts ... which after many devastations, reversals and a very general exhaustion of the state's resources, may accomplish what reason could have suggested to them without so much sad experience, namely: to leave the lawless state of nature and enter into a union of states ...

And no man could say how long this process might take.

At the same time, he believed that the first signs of fundamental improvement in the international practice of states might appear before long. In the *Idea for a Universal History* he noted that civic freedom was already expanding within Europe's states, and attributed this development to the fact that "the states are now on such artificial terms towards each other that not one of them can relax in comparison with the others. Civic freedom cannot now be interfered with without the state feeling the disadvantage ... in all its trades ... and ... a decline of the power of the state in its foreign relations." On the other hand, the economic rivalry of the states was producing closer economic relations between them and rendering their existing attitudes to foreign relations still more artificial, so that it was reasonable to suppose that the beginning of the long process which would ultimately "produce harmony from the very disharmony of men, even against their will", would not be long delayed. It was already possible to envisage a situation in which

the effect of each impact of a government upon other governments in our continent, where states have become so much linked by commerce, will become so noticeable that the other states, compelled by their own danger, will offer themselves as arbiters even when lacking a legal basis, and thus start a future great government of which there is no previous example in history.

Nor was Kant's instinct at fault. Even when he wrote these words the character of international relations in Europe was undergoing a major change, as may be illustrated by the rise of a new attitude towards the balance of power.

As a principle of state—the principle which recommends that states should attend to the international distribution of power when selecting and timing their international decisions—the balance of power has been known, as we have already suggested, in every international system. Indeed, its pursuit is as instinctive as its expediency is obvious within any collection of states. It is not in their familiarity with the principle that we should expect international systems to have varied, so much as in the purposes to which they have applied it. It is true that from about 1600, and especially from the 1640s, governments appear to have become far more familiar with it, and far more articulate about it, if only in Europe, than had ever been the case before—true, too, that this development was too marked to be dismissed as an illusion due simply to the improvement which was taking place in the making and preserving of government records. But even if it was also due to the increase in the complexity of interstate relations, which was also rapid from that time, it was still unaccompanied by any significant change in the way in which states reasoned about the purpose of the balance of power. If we strip down what they now said on this subject in their dispatches, state papers and treaties we find that it amounted to no more than what had been said by the ancient Greeks, or by Machiavelli, who at the end of the fifteenth century had himself still stood "with both feet in the ancient world".[1]

They were perhaps more ingenious than their predecessors in suggesting that some ways of employing the balance of power were cleverer than others, and more subtle in diagnosing the situations and the opportunities which favoured its use. Fundamentally, however, their conclusions still revolved around one or other of two old adages or maxims: safety in numbers; and divide and rule. The balance of power was still thought of only as a rule

[1] Butterfield, H. (London, 1966), in Herbert Butterfield and Martin Wight (eds), *Diplomatic Investigations*, p. 135.

or principle to be followed by the individual state in a process of permanent vigil and struggle between rival states. No state bent on expansion should neglect to reckon by it, nor any state which was threatened by expansion, and all states were judged to be in one or the other of these categories. Of the possibility that it could be used to render interstate struggle less permanent and less intense — as a principle to be applied for the sake of producing stability within the system of states instead of in the interests of each attacking or defending state — there was little if any recognition by governments.

From the last years of the seventeenth century this new view of the purpose of the balance of power had begun to be advocated outside government circles. Thus Fénelon, Louis XIV's great critic, then urged that the princes of Christendom should form a holy alliance for the maintenance of equilibrium in Europe, the balance of power in this sense being the natural law's own safeguard against the traditional destructive quest for a European monarchy. Fénelon's view that this was the proper function of the balance of power had attained wide currency among writers by the time of Voltaire and Vattel, with whose conception of Europe as an international system it had of course a close affinity.[1] By then, again, governments themselves had begun to subscribe to this view on occasions of particular solemnity and to invoke it in defence of their acts of intervention or aggression. The peace treaties of Utrecht in 1713 had been the first to mention, alongside the concern of the contracting states for "the Peace and Tranquility of the Christian World", the belief that the way to secure this was "in a just Balance of Power (which is the best and most solid foundation of mutual friendship and a lasting general accord)". During the following half-century, however, the need to preserve a just balance was so often advanced by the greater states as the justification for their expansion at one anothers'

---

[1] Thus Voltaire's statement of the view that Europe was "a sort of great republic divided into several states, some monarchical, the others mixed . . ., but all in harmony with each other, all possessing the same religious foundation . . ., all possessing the same principles of public and political law, unknown in other parts of the world . . .", ended by saying that the states were "above all . . . at one in the wise policy of maintaining among themselves as far as possible an equal balance of power". *The Age of Louis XIV* (1951), Chapter 2.

expense, or against smaller powers, that whereas writers from Fénelon to Voltaire and Vattel had advocated the balance of power as a "wise principle", a source of international restraint and a guarantee of peace, from about 1760 writers increasingly dismissed it as "the favourite idea . . . of coffee-house politicians" and deplored it as "the main cause of disturbance, of shock and of explosions".[1] But at just this time, in the aftermath of the Seven Years' War, governments adopted Fénelon's attitude not merely in their pretexts for war and their peace-settlement vows, but to the extent that it began for the first time to influence the objectives of their continuing policies.

In order to account for this change, it is necessary to make a simple distinction. The balance of power as a principle of state is quite a different thing from the distribution of international power, even though the phrase "the balance of power" has been given both of these meanings since early in the seventeenth century. Just as the principle can be used in opposite ways, moreover, in the interest of the individual apprehensive or aggressive state or with the purpose of maintaining stability within an entire system of states, so the distribution of power can move between two extremes. It can be so unequal that there will be no balance in it unless one is constructed. Or it can be so spread that its balance imposes itself on governments, whether governments like it or not. Since the beginning of the eighteenth century the distribution of power in the European continent had been moving from the first into the second of these conditions. Increasingly extensive and expensive war was reducing and exhausting its antique accumulations of dynastic power. New recruits to the number of its leading states were being thrown up by the uneven impact upon different societies of those massive processes, the intellectual revolution and the beginning of industrialisation. By the 1760s, for these reasons and in these ways, Europe was approaching a greater near-equality of effective resources between a larger number of states than it had ever known in its history.[2]

[1] See Butterfield and Wight, *Diplomatic Investigations*, pp. 117, 144, 153, 156, and Gilbert, F. (1961), *To the Farewell Address*, pp. 57–65.
[2] For a fuller discussion, see Hinsley, F. H. (1963), *Power and the Pursuit of Peace*, pp. 173–85.

It was in these circumstances, when the continent's communications were also improving and intercourse between its
states was increasing all the time, that, influenced too by the
earlier shift in the attitude to international relations of writers and
thinkers, governments at last faced the fact that a balance of
power was imposed upon them, and accepted for a generation the
discipline which this entailed.

A further stage was entered — the modern international system was
finally launched — when the leading European governments
brought themselves not merely to accept a balanced distribution
of power from considerations of expediency, but also to manufacture such a distribution and to insist that its maintenance was
the true purpose of the principle of the balance of power and the
first principle of a European public law. They did this when the
fortuitous balanced distribution of the late years of the eighteenth
century had been overthrown by the French Revolution and the
Napoleonic Wars.

Napoleon was the product of a political and social revolution
in which France, alone in Europe, made a dramatic further
advance towards the modern structure of government and society
that was slowly being brought into existence throughout the western world by the scientific and industrial revolutions. Her resulting material primacy tempted him to make his conquests. In his
programme of conquest, moreover, the pent-up resentment of the
French nation at the recent decline in French power was combined
with the more general revulsion of the late eighteenth century
from the international politics of the *ancien régime*. On both
accounts his object was the conscious reversal of every recent
innovation of theory and practice in European international
relations, and what he set up was a cross between the antique
programme of universal monarchy and the ideal single commonwealth which had lost its attraction for men in Europe by the
middle of the eighteenth century, but which had recently
been established in the New World in the form of the United
States of America. But when he fell the innovations had their
revenge.

All the recent developments—the new conception of Europe as an international system; the formulation of modern international law; the experience of an equilibrium of actual power between the leading states; the first signs of a movement by those states towards the belief that the maintenance of that equilibrium was the true purpose of the principle of the balance of power; even the demand for a truly international law—were finally fused in an equally conscious determination by the victor governments to establish a European international system incorporating these innovations, and to pursue policies that would safeguard it against a further overthrow. This is the key to the character of the peace settlement of 1815.

Unlike any earlier general settlement in Europe, that of 1815 positively assisted the states to keep for a century a peace that was broken only by an occasional and localised war. It did not do this because its territorial provisions, amounting to the manufacture of a balanced distribution of power to replace that of the last years of the eighteenth century which Napoleon had destroyed, were more comprehensive than any that had been attempted before. Though they were so, they were also the least lasting of its achievements. It did not do so because in another of its provisions the states adopted a further technical innovation in diplomacy by agreeing "to renew at fixed intervals . . . meetings for the purpose of consulting upon common interests, and for the examination of the measures which at each of these epochs shall be considered most salutary for the repose and prosperity of the Nations and for the maintenance of the peace of Europe". This agreement, the origin of the Congress, Concert or Conference system of the nineteenth century, was more significant than it may seem to be when we look back upon it from the peaks of subsequent experiment with the League of Nations and the United Nations Organisation. But it was not until the 1830s that this system was properly inaugurated, after a period in which the agreement to set it up was the source of bickering rather than of collaboration between the states.

What stabilised international relations during the early difficult years and then, despite the initial difficulties, ensured the final establishment of the Concert of Europe as a useful resort for the

solution of international problems—what, despite many subsequent obstacles, thereafter preserved the Concert for decades as a
device for smoothing and regulating the problems that arose from
inevitable changes in the distribution of power—was a more
fundamental achievement of the settlement, the consolidation of
the new view of the international system that had emerged during
the eighteenth century. The settlement marked the first recognition of it by governments, not merely by theorists and critics of
government, and by all the European governments, not merely
by one or another of them. States had duties as well as rights; and
this was especially true of the great states. Among the duties of the
great states, the primary duty was to limit the pursuit of their
individual interests to a point that was consistent with the maintenance of the stability of the European international system as a
whole. In order to assist them in performing this duty they needed
not only the technique of Concert or Conference, but also the
doctrine that the maintenance of an equilibrium was the first
article of a European international or public law. On these beliefs
consensus between the major states in 1815 and the following
years was complete.

CHAPTER SIX

The Modern Pattern of Peace and War

The modern international system assisted the European states to keep among themselves, after 1815, a peace that was broken only by occasional and local war for a hundred years. It cannot be claimed that it made the prime contribution to this outcome. On the contrary, its own final emergence as a body of assumptions and restraints that was accepted by governments, and not merely advocated by theorists, reflected the influence of processes still more fundamental than those we have so far considered.

These were the processes that were producing the modern pattern of peace and war. In order to understand them we must now ask what war is—what it is that distinguishes it from other forms of struggle between men.

In the first place, war is struggle between *organised groups* of men. How should we otherwise distinguish it from murder by and fighting between individuals? Next, it is *armed* struggle between organised groups of men. We must add this if we are to distinguish it from other forms of organised struggle in which men indulge— from politics, for example, or economic competition. But, over and above these requirements, no definition would be complete which did not recognise that war is a form of organised armed struggle to which, in order to distinguish it from other forms of organised armed struggle, men have invariably applied a rule.

Nowadays when the rules of war are mentioned we think of regulations enjoining the humane treatment of military prisoners, protection for innocent civilians, abstention from the use in war of specified methods and weapons. But interest in such regulations developed only in modern times. Those relating to prisoners of war and civilians had their precursors, indeed, in earlier codes based on chivalry between privileged classes, on the political or economic value of captives worthy of ransom or exchange, and on respect for or fear of the powers and the injunctions of religious authorities. Not until the fifteenth and sixteenth centuries, however, and even then only in Europe, did states begin to expand beyond these early precedents, by treaty and international legislation, under pressure from their reciprocal interest in curbing barbarities, from the requirements of military discipline, and from the trades-union concern of their mercenary soldiers. Not until the seventeenth century, again, did they first agree to restrict the methods and weapons that could be used in combat. Even then, the sole problem to evoke any interest before the nineteenth century was the resort to poison and poisoned weapons, a problem which had already exercised the ancient world and the Middle Ages. Even today, because subsequent regulations governing explosives, gas and the most destructive of weapons have been adopted with various qualifications, poison and poisoned weapons are the only tools of war to be unequivocally prohibited by international law. And what is still more important, these man-made attempts to regulate war have been evaded ever since they were introduced.

It is sometimes said that this failure to limit what the law knows as the *ius in bello* is easily enough explained if we remember that before the sixteenth century international systems were too undeveloped to be capable of producing limitations; that during the seventeenth and eighteenth centuries such rules as were produced were inoperable for lack of adequate state controls; that later, from the middle of the nineteenth century, except perhaps for those governing the treatment of prisoners of war, they remained inoperable in the wake of a vast increase in the organisation, the weapons and the scale of war. The real explanation is simpler and more obvious. Rules that have sought to civilise the conduct of war have contradicted not only a prior law of necessity in war, where the object is the submission of the enemy, but also the fundamental function of war itself, which is that it justifies violence and authorises homicide.

From this fundamental fact derives the only other fundamental rule of war — the only rule of war other than the law of necessity that has been always and universally followed. At whatever civilisation we look, whatever may be the era or the area that engages our attention, we shall always find that men have resorted to it. It is the rule that war be formally declared — the rule that the move from the condition of peace to the condition of war demands the solemnity, the ritual of declaring war, and that the solemnity and the ritual give a juridical character to that condition.

It will be objected that this rule, also, has been by no means universally observed. What was only a customary rule between states until as late as the Hague Conferences of 1899 and 1907 was then converted into a legal obligation to precede the resort to war by a formal declaration of war, or by an ultimatum with a conditional declaration, precisely because the custom had frequently been neglected. Since that time even this legal obligation has frequently been evaded. But this objection is removed if another consideration is brought into the account, and the fundamental rule of war will then be seen to possess less affinity with man-made rules, which may be broken, than with that different kind of law which, like the laws of thermodynamics, always operates.

This further consideration arises from the function of justifying homicide which war performs. By virtue of this function, the declaration of war has ever had, has never lost, the quality of a unilateral act. It is a domestic or internal decision, not a bilateral or an international arrangement. Its basic purpose is not to advise an adversary that the condition of war is about to begin. In so far as it does this also, this is a secondary purpose and one which, like the rules for controlling the conduct of war, has developed only in modern times. The basic purpose of the declaration of war is to authorise the group or the community which is about to enter the condition of war to exercise the freedom in the use of force which that condition provides — and to reassure it that the condition of war itself is just or justifiable on public grounds.

At this point a more serious difficulty has to be considered. The function of declaring war has been to authorise violence and justify homicide on public grounds. But it is not solely by this method that this end has been sought. Throughout history the same function has been performed by the exercise of the public power in the interest of maintaining domestic public order. Accordingly, while the declaration of war by those who have possessed the public power has always been a unilateral act, the possession of the public power has always constituted an alternative to it. Whenever a group of men has disliked the thought that, since it does not possess the public authority, its activities will otherwise amount to crime or rebellion, it has deemed these activities to be war, even if it has done so by declaring war for itself. Whenever, on the other hand, a group of men has undertaken activities akin to war without declaring war even unilaterally, it has been because it has believed itself to be responsible for maintaining the public order against rebellion or crime. Other men may have refused to agree with it. Some group's crime may be another group's war, as some group's civil war has ever been another group's rebellion. It makes no matter. Even in modern conditions, when international advantages may accrue from being formally at war, the civil power remains as reluctant as ever to concede that it is at war with rebels.

This difficulty scarcely arises if the public authority is strong, and its possession is undisputed. The distinction between the enemy and the rebel or the criminal—the choice between declaring war and exercising the police power—is then easily made. Even in modern times, however, confusion prevails between war and civil war, between civil war and rebellion, between rebellion and crime—these activities, which men have so much interest in distinguishing, merge into one another in fact and in men's minds —whenever the public authority is weak or its possession is disputed.

Until comparatively recently, this confusion was everywhere the normal, if not the permanent, condition of affairs. The problem confronting men was not how to avoid war. It was how to establish it by distinguishing between war and other forms of organised armed violence, and between war and crime.

When violence was endemic both within and between communities the first concern of the public authority was to establish a monopoly of the use of force, so that it alone could authorise the declaration of war and all resorts to force that it did not authorise were accepted as being breaches of its police power. But so long as this monopoly rested mainly on the possession of force, it could be achieved only temporarily, as by successful empires until they were overthrown. On the collapse or in the absence of effective empire, which in any case largely controlled domestic violence by channelling it into external war, no progress whatever could be made until social development had reduced on the one hand the propensity to violence and, on the other, the reliance of the public authority on force.

In western Europe this was the situation from the decline of the Roman Empire to the beginning of modern times. From the end of the tenth century the Church attempted to bring order out of chaos by organising a peace-movement. In the modern sense of the phrase it was no such thing, and its only sustained result was the development of the medieval theory of "just war". Within Christendom it visited ecclesiastical censures indiscriminately against organised armed force of every variety and kind. It imposed penance for participating in what would nowadays be war. Thus in 993 the Frankish bishops imposed penance on all who had been present on either side at the battle of Soissons, while after the battle of Hastings in 1066 the Norman bishops imposed penance of one year for each man killed by any member of the victorious army. But it applied the same punishment to all other uses of force which it judged to be conducted for secular ends or ends which otherwise disregarded the Church's rules—to individual homicide; to attacks on travellers and pilgrims; to any fighting that took place during closed periods of the year. The distinction it drew, indeed, was not that between these other activities and war; it was that between any armed struggle, including war, within Christendom, which it sought to limit, and war on behalf of Christendom, which met with full ecclesiastical approval. Even as the so-called peace-movement was developing in Europe, it was also becoming part of papal teaching that the participants in such a war—a just war against the infidel—were not subject to penance or guilty of homicide should they slay, and were positively meritorious, and assured of general absolution and eternal salvation, should they be slain.

From the middle of the eleventh century this teaching was deepened and broadened with the increase of papal power. On the one hand, participation in just war, from being approved of, was converted into binding duty by the formalisation of the crusader's vow—into a duty, moreover, which the pope could enforce by legal sanctions until its time ran out or the goal was gained. On the other hand, the concept of the just war was stretched beyond forays against Slavs in the east and Moors in Spain, and beyond the crusade itself, to cover armed undertakings within Christendom—against rebels in the Campania; against Norman brigandage in southern Italy; against the Hohenstaufen emperors and the Italian cities; against the Albigensians; against any enemy, indeed, that the Papacy might select. A secular as well as an ecclesiastical power, but one lacking the force of an effective empire, the Papacy was itself driven to ignore the original justification for just war.

At the same time, and for the same reason, the ecclesiastical effort to moderate the resort to armed struggle in secular causes within Europe had failed. From the outset monks had done penance for warriors, and penance by proxy had deprived the Church's censure of its effect. Still more important, the combination of uncertain public authority and undifferentiated disorder had perpetuated the situation in which for every possessor of secular power the road to greater power lay through suppression and conquest. On the other hand, the secular authorities were concerned to retain their power and to maintain order in their territories. By the thirteenth century for these two reasons—in order both to exempt war by rulers from papal censure and to retain that censure upon unofficial war, rebellion and brigandage —just war was coming to betoken any armed struggle by any secular ruler who was recognised by the Church, provided it was not against the Papacy or against an interest which the pope wished to protect. And in order to distinguish it from secular war, papal war was coming to be termed not "just war", but "holy war".

Holy war and just war, the justifications for the ecclesiastical and secular resort to armed force, remained dominant theories from the thirteenth to the sixteenth century. They did so because armed conflict continued to conform to the pattern which, except for temporary interludes, it had obeyed for centuries—to the pattern in which public and private war, interstate war and civil war, civil war and rebellion, rebellion and brigandage, were inextricably mingled, and more or less continuous. If this was the case in Europe there is every reason for believing that it was also the case elsewhere. It was only in Europe, on the other hand, that, beginning in the sixteenth century and culminating in the eighteenth, a quite different pattern of armed struggle began to assert itself.

The new pattern derived from two developments. The first was a pronounced movement towards the monopolisation by the state of the resort to armed force, and thus towards the differentiation of interstate war from other forms of conflict and the canalisation of conflict into interstate war.

Civil war and revolution did not cease to take place in Europe and the societies intimately connected with it. On the contrary, as the English Civil War, the American Revolution, the French Revolution, the American Civil War and the Russian Revolution and Civil War bear witness, they now acquired an enhanced significance, both in themselves and in the history books. But these great events of modern times owed some at least of their importance to the fact that, when the first of them took place, revolution and civil war were coming to be abnormal, not common, occurrences. As compared with most of their forerunners, again, they were larger in scale because they had ceased to be outcrops of endemic but localised and separatist resistance to the centralising state, or incidents in a perpetual round of palace intrigue, and were becoming efforts to abolish the palace and take over the entire machinery of the state itself, usually with the intention of accelerating its centralising work. The decline in the frequency of revolution and civil war was associated with a change in their relation to the state. It was a change that carried over to the lesser forms of organised violence there — to insurgency and brigandage — and that brought about, if not their extinction, at least their reduction from the end of the eighteenth century to dimensions which called forth the beginning of the modern police.

This development was before long followed by another. The first effect of the state's growing monopoly of armed force within society was an increase in the frequency of interstate war. By the seventeenth century there were only seven years in the whole century (1610, 1669–71, 1680–2) when interstate war was not taking place somewhere in Europe. But by the closing years of the eighteenth century, at least between the major states, we can detect the emergence of a marked alternation of long periods of peace with short bursts of war. In contrast to the earlier condition of affairs in which interstate war had become a nearly continuous if limited activity — a natural occupation interrupted regularly by the winter season, but rarely by such considerations as financial stringency or political prudence — this alternation has ever since the eighteenth century been the most persistent and the most characteristic feature in the relations between the leading states. Between 1763 and the wars that followed the French Revolution there were, for the first time, as many as thirty years of almost total peace between these states. There were forty years of peace between them between 1815 and 1854; forty-four years between 1871 and 1914; twenty years between 1918 and 1939. And since 1945, again, there have already been another twenty-seven years of peace between the Great Powers in an international system which has ceased to be a European system and become world-wide.

We must not exaggerate the decisiveness of these two shifts. Modern police forces were not fully established before the middle of the nineteenth century. It was not until then, again, that states were able finally to abandon a system which had operated since the Middle Ages and which had been a compromise between their anxiety to establish their monopoly of peace and war and the fact that their control was far from complete — the system by which, by issuing letters of marque and authorising individual retaliation and reprisals, they had licensed private war against the inhabitants of other states. As late as the end of the nineteenth century not even the most sophisticated of the states could control their nationals beyond a certain distance from their capitals — could prevent a Cecil Rhodes or officers of the French North African commands, let alone Russian generals in the Manchurian area, from fighting campaigns and creating empires with almost as much freedom as the Conquistadores. The periods of peace after the 1760s were marked not only by wars between the great states and lesser powers, but also by frequent clashes involving the danger of war between the great states themselves. At the other extreme, various developments — the change from land-based wealth to a money economy, for example; the rise of artillery; the appearance of nationalist sentiment; even the Tudor revolution in government — had been producing a slow movement from the periphery to the centre since as early as the fifteenth century, at least in some of Europe's societies. Even so, we shall not go far wrong if we conclude that it was the eighteenth century which constituted the great turning-point.

When we ask why these developments took place, this fact becomes understandable. Up to the eighteenth century, even in the most advanced of Europe's societies, provincial divisions and local structures had everywhere remained so strong, and systems of government, organisational techniques, state frontiers and communications had remained so primitive and unsettled, that there was little approach to that central state regulation of society and of the resort to force which largely explains both the modern alternation of peace and war in the relations between states and the reduced frequency, if also the greater scale, of domestic disruption. Beginning in the eighteenth century, on the other hand, three basic processes — the closer consolidation and integration of the political community; the accompanying rise of organised government, of the modern state, within the community; the underlying advance of science and technology — have made continuous inroads into that earlier situation.

It was then that, after previously moving forward at a slow pace, erratically, and with only limited effect, these processes underwent

the leap forward or "take-off" which has given a dynamic, inter-
locking quality to their subsequent advance, and compounded
their social, political, economic and intellectual impact. Nor is it
inappropriate to borrow the analogy of "take-off" from the
economists.

It was in the eighteenth century that, as well as becoming fused,
the processes were rearranged in such a way as to bring to the
forefront that one among them which had previously been least
prominent, but which, with the proliferation of science and the
rise of technology, produced the first industrial revolution. It was
in the eighteenth century, again, that they first produced the shift
in terminology, in concepts, in attitudes which, just as much as
the first industrial revolution, divides the societies and the institutions of the modern world from those of the pre-industrial ages.

At the end of the seventeenth century, to take but one example,
it was not only the case that, even in Europe, no state drew up a
modern budget, organised a modern national debt, and planned
and controlled in the modern way the national finance and
revenues. In no state did even the conception of a budget or of the
national debt or of financial planning exist, and no government
possessed the knowledge on which these notions could be formed.
None knew how much revenue there was, or how much debt,
and none thought it possible or necessary to know. War was
waged with loans raised at very high interest, and government
bankruptcy was the almost inevitable accompaniment or consequence of war. But by the end of the eighteenth century, at least
in the more advanced of Europe's societies, these concepts had
everywhere become established, and the appropriate institutional
changes were beginning to be made. It is not without significance
that from the 1760s France began to lag behind in a widespread
move towards that public management of public resources of
which the absolute monarchies, no less than medieval rulers, had
scarcely felt the need, but that one of the consequences of the
French Revolution was the greater centralisation of the resources
of the French nation by the state.

Another of its consequences was to reveal for the first time the
effect of the better organisation of government and the greater

articulation of the community upon the scale of war. The modern pattern of peace and war has not only consisted of an alternation of long periods of peace with short bursts of war; beginning with the wars that followed the French Revolution, it has also been the case that, as never before, war was always liable to be more intensive and extensive every time it recurred. If the emergence of the modern pattern was partly due to the improved control which governments were acquiring over the resort to war, it also reflected their greater reluctance to accept the destructiveness and the hazards which these wars had involved.

The drift towards the total commitment of society in the event of war was resisted by governments during the next fifty years, from fear of its consequences as well as from the fact that they were on their guard against the danger of internal revolution. In the next period of hostilities between the industrialising societies, between 1854 and 1871, though the wars were fought at a higher level of potential destructiveness than ever before, they were also fought by largely professional armies in limited and, as far as possible, lightning campaigns. But the American Civil War was already indicating what would result when this trend escaped control, as from the 1870s, in the wake of a massive acceleration of the movement towards modern society and the modern state, it did.

From that date, as we shall see in more detail later on, armies finally ceased to be professional corporations, distinct from society. War finally ceased to be a form of gladiatorial combat. At least in wars between industrial societies and modern states, victory ceased to require only the military defeat of an opposing army. It came to depend on the total destruction of the opposing society's will to fight on, and this called for the complete reduction of its fabric and resources. At the same time, the application of science and technology to the weapons of war, continuous since the eighteenth century, was also greatly accelerated, thus raising the extent and the level of destruction that a society could withstand and that it must be prepared to impose.

If these developments reinforced the growing reluctance of governments to accept the risks of war, while at the same time increasing their ability to regulate the resort to it, the same was

true of the ever-sharper contrast which they were setting up between the condition of war and the condition of peace. Up to the
eighteenth century armed conflict had been more or less continuous within and between societies but, being based on a limited
and a little-changing technology, it had also been restricted in
scale. In addition, however, it had been conducted within a
primitive framework of social arrangements. Natural disasters,
famine, poverty and pestilence, all beyond human control, had
been the main sources of misery. War had done no more than
accentuate the misery, and, as it had been an alternative to other
forms of conflict, so it could be an antidote to despair. But from
the end of the eighteenth century, and progressively during the
nineteenth century, the scale and destructiveness of war were
mounting at a time when the better integration of societies and
the increasing efficiency of states were providing men for the first
time with an ever-growing capacity to limit natural disasters and
improve social conditions.

The fact that the destructiveness of war and the power to control other scourges were both increasing simultaneously undoubtedly changed the general climate of opinion. If "the idea of
controlling wars, like the idea of the emancipation of women and
the idea of birth control, is part of the intellectual revolution of
the 19th century", this, rather than the fact that historians had
until then "remained under the influence of Greek and Roman
historiography", was the fundamental reason. But if scholars now
ceased to accept war "as a natural fact about which nothing could
be done" — if "the phenomenon of war as such, its place in human
life, its relation to political and economic forms, the possibility of
avoiding it, not just of postponing it to a better moment",[1] were
now seriously studied for the first time — we may be sure that
governments were also responding to this change in the relation of
war to society, and that this was no less influential than the change
in the character of society and the change in the scale of war in
enabling them to establish the modern alternation of war and
peace.

[1] For the quotations in this paragraph, see A. D. Momigliano (London, 1966),
Studies in Historiography, pp. 120, 123–4.

CHAPTER SEVEN

The Collapse of the Modern International System

If only in the industrialising societies, the processes which produced the modern pattern of peace and war also brought governments to adopt the attitudes and arrangements which constituted the modern international system. Not even between those societies did this system accomplish what, unlike previous international systems, it had been designed to achieve. Though at longer intervals than before, peace continued to break down; eventually it broke down so completely that the system was itself destroyed. Why did it do so?

It might seem that we should answer this question by resolving a fundamental uncertainty about the causes of war. There would be no need for further explanation if we could show that it was not to be expected that the shift towards modern government and society would eliminate war—or the rise of the modern international system or, even, the conjunction of these two vast changes—because war is unavoidable: that—though in different conditions it may fall into different patterns, as it may assume different forms—whatever the conditions, it must recur. Alternatively, the answer would present no problems if we could show that, at least in the modern conditions, war "broke out" only when some government or governments preferred it to some other course.

But when we study the controversy which still surrounds the causes of every modern war we soon recognise two things. In the last resort, the conflicting interpretations rest on these rival assumptions.[1] And the controversy continues because, despite the fact that men have debated since the beginning of the nineteenth century the causes of war as such, and not merely the causes of individual wars, these assumptions remain assumptions — unverifiable and incapable of being refuted.[2]

Each, of course, has something of a negative argument in its favour. On the one hand, the fact that wars may appear to have resulted from precise motives and deliberate policies does not invalidate the belief that they have really arisen because governments and societies have been unable to avoid them. In early modern Europe, we could as easily maintain, it was just because the state was increasingly channelling the natural urge to violence into restricted forms and selected directions — just because it was replacing an earlier confused struggle of all against all by delimiting hostilities as to time and enemy and object — that wars were so frequent. And in the modern international system, in much the same way, the fact that war occurred at longer intervals than before may reflect the fact that, while men had become freer when deciding whether and when to fight, they still were not free not to indulge in war from time to time.

This conclusion might explain, indeed, why modern wars have increasingly assumed the character of being a form of pathological release. If men's aggressive impulses were being bottled up by the modern state and the operation of the modern international system at just the time when they were also becoming more organised in the wake of the increasing integration of societies, this would account for some of the characteristics of modern

[1] Thus, those who maintain that the First and Second World Wars were caused by the truculent or aggressive policies of Germany's governments adopt the second assumption. On the other hand, those who lean to the first assumption argue either that all the governments involved were helpless — or fallible: it comes to the same thing — or that, if Germany was more aggressive than the others, it was no more so than the others would have been in its more difficult — or more powerful: again it comes to the same thing — situation.

[2] It is no doubt on this account that they are adopted implicitly, without being explicitly stated. Certainly, the tendency to rest on one or the other of these positions without stating that it is being accepted is one of the things which increases the confusion of the debate in which, while German "revisionist" historians are now dedicated to overturning the almost unanimous conviction of their predecessors by urging that the Kaiser's government was just as responsible for the war of 1914 as was Hitler's for the war of 1939, British "revisionist" historians are beginning to insist that Hitler's government was not responsible for the war of 1939.

nationalism. We cannot overlook the evidence that from the time when the outbreak of the Crimean War closed the first long period of peace—and men first rejoiced, in Tennyson's words, that "the long, long canker of peace" was over—every further stretch of international stability was accompanied by a rising tide of readiness for the excitement of war. But neither can we dismiss, on this kind of evidence, the view that wars have been the outcome of decision, calculation and policy.

Against the argument that the stated reasons for which they have been declared have been merely pretexts, the discoverable motives for them merely rationalisations, and that we can throw no light on their causes by investigating these merely superficial aspects—the top of the iceberg—it may be urged that, of all social activities, war is the one that carries the highest risks, requires the highest degree of preparation, and demands the highest degree of resolution. Not for nothing is it begun with solemnities and conducted against precise enemies on precise issues. Is it not probable that, far from being the unavoidable outcome of men's impulses, it must always have been the deliberate outcome of men's will?

It may be true that before the eighteenth century the risks and the preparation involved in war were so little raised above those attached to normal existence that war was a natural activity. It does not follow that, even then, it was unavoidable in the sense that it broke out whether states wanted it or not. An equally plausible view is that it did so because states had no interest in avoiding it and, being geared to war, no adequate devices for avoiding it. From the end of the eighteenth century the risks involved in war began to mount, and its preparation and organisation became ever more complex, so that it ceased to be a natural activity, at least in the more advanced societies. At the same time it became less frequent between those societies. Plainly, this reflected the fact that, when the decision to embark on it was becoming more difficult than ever before, they were developing an interest in avoiding it, and devices to assist them in doing so. But is it not even clearer than before that in this situation war only occurred when, as well as deciding on war, some government or governments also willed it?

Unfortunately this conclusion does not follow, either. It is possible that, if the devices proved to be inadequate, it was for this reason—that the interest in avoiding war was less strong, at intervals, than the will to have war. But it is no less possible that they were inadequate against forces and pressures by which, if less frequently than before, governments continued to be overwhelmed. It cannot be excluded, indeed, that the modern international system collapsed for both of these reasons. If these assumptions about the causes of war are rival assumptions, in the sense that they represent the extremes between which all conclusions on the subject must come to rest, they are not necessarily mutually exclusive. And it is perhaps on this account that they remain assumptions.

What follows, then, is the need to adopt a different approach. We must ask not why war continued in the modern international system, but in what ways did the system fall short of what was required if war was to be avoided in the modern situation. To what strains, in fact, was the system subjected? And what were its limitations, as revealed by those strains?

To turn to the first of these enquiries is to be reminded of the fundamental importance in modern times of those three processes which have continually gathered momentum since the eighteenth century—the movement of political communities towards greater integration, the rise within the political community of the regulatory state, and the continuing march of technology. For it is another feature of modern times, no less fundamental in importance, that these developments have not taken place throughout the world; even where they have proceeded, moreover, they have not taken place to the same extent and at the same speed. And it is the fact that they affected different political communities disproportionately, unevenly, in a world in which they were also conspiring to make all political communities more closely interlocked—it is this fact which set up the strains that the modern international system was unable to absorb, and which governed the extent of them.

We have noticed already that the uneven advance of these

developments within Europe, to which at first their impact was confined, created to begin with, not strain, but a greater international stability than that area had known since the collapse of Rome. From the middle of the eighteenth century the greater rapidity of advance in these directions of some European communities as compared with others had the effect of levelling up an old dynastically-accumulated and highly unstable distribution of power. It is to this effect that we may attribute the comparative composure of the modern international system during the first century of its existence—to about 1860.

The phenomenon of the French Revolution and Napoleon, an interlude in this composure, is not a refutation of this argument. It was precisely because the French Revolution accomplished, alone in France, a further and a startling stride towards the integrated nation and the modern state that the new balance of the last years of the eighteenth century was disturbed. Because the Revolution accomplished this only on the political level, Napoleon reverted to the goal of primitive empire, which the great states in Europe had but recently relinquished. Napoleon's imperialism, however, invested the new balance with a new virtue in the eyes of other states. This induced them to buttress their restoration of it with the attitudes and the policies which constituted the modern international system in the last resort, and which added to stability after 1815. But from the 1850s the disproportionate advance of the processes that were increasingly moving the criteria of power towards bureaucratic, industrial and scientific ability, and that were giving added importance to the degree of national integration, began to produce distortions in the distribution of power which had been stable, and which government had succeeded in keeping stable, for forty years.

At first, unlike those produced by the French Revolution, the distortions which now appeared were not acute. As between Europe and the outside world, on most of which the processes had still made no impact, they did indeed become wide. It was this fact which underlay the great burst of modern colonialism that took place when the extended technical reach of the European societies met with the stagnant political and social condition of the extra-European lands. Between the European societies themselves, however, colonialism, while it led to much bickering and even more diplomatic activity, produced no danger of war. The initial breakdowns in the modern international system—the European wars of the period between 1854 and 1870—were generated wholly by the fact that Europe itself was shifting away from the rough equality of strength which had been re-established on the fall of Napoleon. They were restricted breakdowns because the shift was as yet slight. They were also restricted—by no means irreparable— because they arose between states which sought not to destroy the international system, but to accommodate it by limited, if forcible, adjustments to the shift. Whatever the other differences between them, this much was common to the policies of Bismarck, Cavour and Napoleon III.

From the 1870s, on the other hand, the rate of advance of the fundamental developments most markedly accelerated, and the speed and effect of their advance became increasingly dispropor- tionate even as between the European societies, according to the differences between them in previous history, in social structure, and in their involvement in what had now become an inter- national economy. It is to these facts that we may safely attribute the grave unsettlement of that period in the history of the modern international system which began in the 1890s, witnessed the First World War and lasted till the conclusion of the Second World War—of the period which was ushered in by the unification of Germany and closed by the destruction, upon her second defeat, of the greatest degree of material primacy that any state had possessed on the European continent since the days of Napoleon.

It was not only from within that the European international system was now subjected to enormous strain. Also from the 1870s, these developments—the integration of the community, the rise of modern government, the advance of industry, technology and science—were producing beyond Europe not merely the intensi- fication of European colonialisation but, now for the first time, new centres of great power. In the United States after the Civil War of the 1860s and in Japan after the Meiji revolution of the same time, and after the defeat in 1871 of the last feudal rebellion there, they were producing, indeed, steadily and inexorably, by the application of their powerful stimulus to indigenous material and human resources, what were to be greater separate centres of power than Europe was capable of harbouring. Already by the 1900s, by the relevant criteria of international power, the United States was overtopping the whole of western Europe, and in the Russo-Japanese war Japan defeated a European power. Nor was Russia herself to remain a purely European power for much longer. Since the abolition of serfdom, also in the 1860s, she too had at last embarked on the modernisation of her economy and society. By the 1880s she had reached a rate of industrial growth that was as high as any in the world and that was to bring her, after some delay and much tribulation, to within measurable distance of the combined strength of the remainder of Europe.

It is scarcely possible to over-estimate the rapidity, the novelty and the scale of these changes. They took place essentially within a man's lifetime. Their novelty was such that, while we dare not say that it will never again be paralleled, we may safely affirm that it had never previously been approached. In scale they constituted so huge a redistribution of power as either to necessitate an equally rapid and large expansion of the European international system, if stability was to be preserved, or to threaten the system with destruction.

In the event, its timely expansion proved impossible. And all the more was this the case because of another development involving technology and the closer organisation of society. If the distribution of power was in an especially unstable stage of transition during the half-century after 1890, so was the movement towards the greater complexity of weapons. This had steadily gathered momentum since the early decades of the nineteenth century. From the 1870s its momentum greatly accelerated. Effective weapon ranges, ten times greater in 1870 than in 1815, were forty times greater by 1900. Until 1945, however, the effect of this technological advance piled up within the boundaries of two great limiting factors.

On the one hand, the most deadly of weapons could still be

effectively brought to bear, and could still be effectively countered, only by organising ever-larger war plans for deploying ever-larger masses of men. Before the 1870s it had been rare for an army to exceed 250,000 men. In 1900 France and Germany could put $3\frac{1}{2}$ million men into the field, and Russia 4 million, and they had no choice but to be ready to do so. The combination of the decline of tactical mobility on the battlefield, as a result of the increasing heaviness and deadliness of weapons, with the impact of the railway in increasing strategic mobility—the ability to deploy masses of men and arms on a front, and to switch them from front to front—was erecting mass and mechanical attrition, on a dreadful scale, into the centre-piece of battle, even as the rapidly growing integration, articulation and regulation of societies were making the exhaustion of the adversary's national resources, and its national will to fight on, the ultimate and inescapable objective in war.

On the other hand, the increase in the efficiency of weapons and in the required and possible size of armies was not yet creating the overwhelming and universal deterrent force against the readiness to accept the risk of war with which, if only as between the most advanced states, armaments have come to be invested since the development from the 1940s of the atomic and nuclear bombs. That the increase was having some deterrent effect well before 1914 is clear. The outstanding feature of the system of alliances that grew up alongside the armaments revolution after the 1870s was that, unlike earlier such systems, it was composed of alliances which were all defensive. Initially, by co-ordinating the forces of two or more armies that were more massive and mobile than ever before, their object was to deter another such army from risking the attack which, given its increasing mass and mobility, was increasingly difficult to counter. But it is equally clear that before 1939 the deterrent effect was by no means overwhelming, and that acceleration of the weapons and scale of war was all the more dangerous on that account.

In Europe before 1914 the widespread delusion that a war would be won and lost in a few months was not based on ignorance of the probable consequences of this acceleration should war break out. The publics of the time may have remained unaware of these consequences, but among governments the delusion was the outcome of the desperate wishful thinking of experts who were only too well aware that, unless a war were won at once, by a lightning stroke, it could not be won at all in the new conditions without even the victor incurring almost insupportable damage. So great was this awareness, however, that in the years immediately before the First World War it produced, together with the delusion, the increasing temptation to break through the deterrent circle of the alliances with a preventive war—just as during that war it produced increasingly futile efforts, especially in non-continental Great Britain, to mount peripheral campaigns as a means of escaping the logic of a conflict that was doomed to be decided in a trial of endurance on the western front.

Between 1919 and 1939 the atmosphere in Europe was even more disturbed, the situation even more brittle, because the belief in the feasibility of a brief and comparatively painless war was abandoned by some governments but not by all. Some governments, recoiling from the horrors of the western front, said "Never again", and buttressed their determination to avoid a further war by exaggerating the power of further technological developments like the bomber to intensify the movement to attrition and annihilation which had ended in the trenches in the previous war. Others, welcoming these further developments as at last creating the means of escape from war by mass and attrition, rationalised the delusion by adopting the technique of *blitzkrieg*, the doctrine of war of movement and the strategy of indirect approach, and they were encouraged to do so by the most advanced strategists of the day.

No less disturbing was the fact that throughout those years, before both of the World Wars, the development of weapons had consequences for the European states different from those which they had for the powers which were emerging beyond the European continent. When weapons and war were becoming continental in their range, especially after the development of air power, no state in Europe, however great its reluctance, could avoid involvement in the deteriorating situation there. Hence the demise of Great Britain's tradition of "splendid isolation" from the first years of this century. But in circumstances in which even the range of air power remained limited to a continent, no state beyond Europe would contemplate the massive preparation which, in view of the risk of war, involvement in European affairs would entail.

After the outbreak of war in 1914 the resources of the United States and Japan were indeed added to those which, in Europe itself, had been inadequate to contain Germany's growth in power; but before 1914, while Japan had remained of peripheral importance, the United States had increasingly insisted on her isolationist tradition. From 1905, when Great Britain began to be more deeply engaged than had been her custom in the European situation, the Anglo-Japanese alliance, originally concluded in 1902 to protect the interests of the two Powers in the Far East, enabled her to concentrate her naval forces in home waters. But Japan's interest in the alliance remained the consolidation and extension of her influence in the Far East, which was also her sole concern in participating in the First World War and at the 1919 peace conference.

After the outbreak of war in 1939, again, the extra-European resources of the United States and Russia were eventually thrown in to bring about the defeat of Germany and restore a balance in Europe. Before the Second World War, however, these outside powers had kept their distance from the problems of the European states. Russia, forced into temporary eclipse as a power by her continuing revolution, was now divorced from them not only by the military risks of involvement, but also by the ideological gulf which that revolution had opened up between her and the rest of the world. After the intervention of the United States in the First World War her isolationism was even more intense. In addition, her long-standing dislike of the Anglo-Japanese alliance was perhaps decisive in severing, within a few years of the end of the First World War, the tenuous link which had earlier been forged between Europe and Japan.

Faced with an unstable — and after 1919 an explosive — situation, the European international system was thus unable to meet it by calling in new worlds to redress the balance of the old, and it was only after the Second World War, and even then only haltingly, that the leading extra-European powers and the old states of Europe were to be merged into an international system that was global in its range. Until then, the equilibrium between the European states was passing away just when international disorder was beginning to involve alliances and military preparation on an unprecedented scale. And just when the maintenance of equilibrium in Europe was, even so, ceasing to be possible by reference to Europe alone—just when its states were having to measure themselves against powers that were emerging beyond the continent and, in the case of Russia, against a state that was graduating from the status of a European state to that of a power on a continental scale—these alliances and this preparation were not only confining the horizon of the European states to Europe, but were also reinforcing the historical and geographical isolation from Europe of the extra-European powers. But these strains were also revealing that the modern or the European system had another serious limitation.

During the first half of the nineteenth century the system had evolved on the basis of the two great innovations which had been prepared by developments in the eighteenth century and completed during the Napoleonic Wars: the diplomatic contrivance of a Congress or a Concert of the leading states, and an ideological climate in which those states agreed, as never before, on the necessity of working together in the interest of avoiding further war. At first, its evolution had been delayed by differences of interests and ideas. In the 1820s it well-nigh collapsed, not least because of the initial association of the Congress or the Concert in the minds of some of the governments with the antique aspiration of establishing a federation of Europe and with their post-war programme of suppressing the Revolution by intervening in the internal affairs of states—with the preoccupations, in fact, of the Holy Alliance to which other governments were opposed. So strong, however, was the concensus on the central issue of peace that by 1831 the Concert was freed of these associations, and was firmly accepted by all the Great Powers as a strictly international device for assisting them to solve or contain strictly international problems without recourse to war. More than that, it was acquiring a new association—the association with the idea that its international political operations were informed and sanctioned by a public law.

"Each nation has its rights, but Europe also has its rights", declared one of the protocols of the conference summoned in that year to settle the future of Belgium. By 1856 this vague formula had hardened into "the Public Law and System (Concert) of Europe" which the Treaty of Paris announced as being the basis of its validity. But if the Congress of Paris saw the endowment of the Concert with an international theory, it also registered the high-water mark of its development as an international system. Coming at the close of the Crimean War, in which some of the Great Powers had fought each other, and at the outset of the movement of Europe away from the actual balance of power between its states, which had been established in 1815, it opened a period in which the Powers became increasingly unwilling or unable to operate the system's central technical device. International conferences were not resorted to even to ratify the results of the European wars which were fought between 1859 and 1871, let alone in advance of them, in an effort to avert them. More important still—for, despite this fact, the Concert machinery was revived in 1878 by the Congress of Berlin, and it continued to prove useful at intervals from then until 1913—the Congress of Paris revealed that the Concert system was incapable of evolving an adequate public law.

We have already noticed the principles on which it rested. The Great Powers shared a common responsibility for maintaining the peace of Europe. To that end, problems should be solved and changes made not by one or some of the Powers, but only with the concurrence of all. Further, since states find it easier to accept generalities than to apply them in particular cases, the need for a practical test of whether solutions and changes were equitable and tolerable was supplied by the principle of the balance of power. Ideally, the settlement laid down in the treaties of 1815 should be preserved; if it had to be modified, it was understood that the changes should be as limited as circumstances allowed, and offset by compensations which in practice kept a balance intact.

So far as they went these principles were enlightened enough. Even the third, the least high-sounding and thus the most open to disputed interpretation, represented a great advance: it replaced the autonomous and expansionist use of the balance of power by the commonly accepted doctrine that the function of the balance of power was the maintenance of international stability. Down to the middle of the nineteenth century, moreover, so long as the actual distribution of power in Europe remained reasonably stable, they made possible not only the diplomatic settlement of international disputes, but also the consolidation and the extension of the customary rules of international law. But at that point, and in the course of this development, they conflicted with an older principle which proved to be more powerful.

The rules of existing international law — rules enjoining good faith, defining international responsibility, regulating the recognition of states, establishing the freedom of the seas — all stemmed from the fundamental principle of the sovereignty of the state. Between 1815 and 1856 the Concert system succeeded in breaching this principle in a few directions — by laying down rules governing diplomatic precedence, for example, and by establishing free navigation of international rivers. It did not even attempt to breach it as its central point, which was the right of the state to go to war not merely in self-defence but for any reason whatever. In 1856 itself the Peace Movement hoped that the Congress of Paris would adopt "some system of international arbitration which may bring the greatest interest of nations within the cognisance of certain fixed rules of justice and right". But the Congress confined itself, in Protocol 23 to the Treaty of Paris, to expressing the desire that states "should, before appealing to arms, have recourse, as far as circumstances allow, to the good offices of a friendly power". At the Hague Conferences of 1899 and 1907 this first experience was repeated. At each of these conferences the first Convention drew attention, indeed, to arbitration, as well as to mediation and good offices, as methods by which states might settle their differences peacefully. But it also laid down that these were purely optional alternatives to war, available if states were minded to use them.

The international law of the modern international system thus registered no advance beyond that of earlier systems on this central issue. While every sovereign state continued to hold as of right whatever it possessed, every sovereign state continued to be entitled to challenge the existing order by invoking an unlimited *jus ad bellum*. Changes to that order might be the outcome of unilateral resort to force and duress, but they were also the outcome of this right, and they were legitimised by virtue of its universal recognition. It is arguable indeed that this right to war was now less questioned than before, as the business of interpreting the rules of law, becoming more professional, lost its association with theology and morality. Certainly, none of the growing body of international legal writers ever questioned it down to 1918. All of them defined peace in negative terms as "the termination of war" —as that legal condition of relations which was peace because the states involved considered it to be not the legal condition of belligerency, involving special privileges against third parties and the international system as a whole as well as against the selected enemy, which every state had the individual right to invoke. As late as 1924 they commonly held with regard to this right that "international law has no alternative but to accept war, independently of the justice of its origin, as a relation which the parties to it may set up, if they choose, and to busy itself only in regulating the effect of the relation . . . Hence both parties to every war are regarded as being in an identical legal position, and consequently as being possessed of equal rights."[1]

This being so, the *jus ad bellum* being unimpaired in practice and unchallenged by legal theory, it was ultimately of little avail that states were more restrained than before in their resort to it. Despite the fact that the modern international system incorporated significant advances on other fronts, its retention of this right dictated its failure to preserve the peace, even if it also revealed that its prime object was not to preserve the peace but to preserve

[1] Hall, W. E. (8th edn, 1924), *International Law*, p. 82.

international stability. Between 1856 and 1871, though the Great Powers restricted the objectives of their wars, from a continuing respect for the stabilising influence of the balance of power, they abandoned the contrivance of the Concert and the principles which underlay it, those principles which said that they had the duty to work together to maintain peace. During the 1870s and the 1880s they temporarily revived the Concert, a new balance having been brought into existence, but they did not fully return to its underlying principles. Just as they developed competing alliances alongside the Concert, so instead of returning to its principles, they reduced their concept of the public law of Europe until it meant no more than reliance on the balance between their alliances.

After the 1890s, as the competition between the alliances increased and as dissatisfaction with the new balance of power began to spread, the very idea of a European public law died altogether. Competition for power, justified by the balance of power, and offset only by their growing reluctance to fight, was the only rule of conduct in a society of states which, as was confirmed in 1914, had no true public law beyond the right to war of the individual sovereign state. Nor did this situation change before 1939, when, despite a radical but perhaps also a premature attempt to improve it, the modern international system foundered in yet another World War.

CHAPTER EIGHT

The Search for Peace in the First Half of the Twentieth Century

At the beginning of the nineteenth century, during the first of the modern periods of war, all the conceptual changes of the eighteenth century, all the resulting criticism of established international practice, all the most pressing interests of governments themselves, had finally combined to produce the modern international system. From the beginning of the twentieth century a similar process was repeated. During the next fifty years, when that system was staggering to its end, the prime problem in international history was the question whether men could devise a better system to take its place.

The stultification of the modern international system after the 1870s had coincided with vast social changes, which were producing mass semi-literate electorates as well as mass armies, and ideological trends like neo-Hegelianism and social-Darwinism which accepted the need for — which even applauded — struggle and war between the system's increasingly powerful states. But attitudes began to change from the early 1900s when international tension again spilled over into diplomatic crises and what men then called, not cold, but dry war. The ranks of the modern Peace Movement, which had been founded at the close of the Napoleonic Wars but which had languished since the Crimean War, were swelled by new groups of critics of the international system, and national peace congresses or executive committees were established in country after country to co-ordinate their increasingly varied activities. With the outbreak of major war, in 1914, what had nevertheless remained the concern of minorities became the concern of many more. At the end of the First World War governments themselves embarked on a determined attempt to rectify the system's proven inability to avoid war.

At the end of the Second World War their efforts had to be renewed: their outcome, the League of Nations, unlike the Concert system of the nineteenth century, had ended in early as well as in total failure. Its failure had been most complete in just those directions where the Concert system had shown that the need for advance was most acute. It had been all the more pronounced because in some other directions the League of Nations had been effective.

It would be an exaggeration to claim that in its capacity as a standing international organisation to supervise existing legislative and administrative international arrangements, and to facilitate the making of more, its establishment greatly stimulated international collaboration. In this direction it was so much a natural, not to say a practically unavoidable, extension of a movement that had long been gathering force that, if a more ambitious League had not incidentally assumed it, some organisation would in any case have been created to perform this function.

Ever since the middle of the nineteenth century *ad hoc* international conferences had been convened with some regularity to enact new international law on such subjects as maritime warfare, the treatment of prisoners, and the declaration of war. Beginning with the International Telegraphic Union in 1865, international institutions and agreements, aimed at co-ordinating and standardising national law on administrative matters which respected no frontiers—on disease and public health; on copyright; on postal, cable and other communications—had also become increasingly common. With the continual increase in the integration of societies, the spread of technology and the expansion of the domestic functions of the state, governments were discovering that they could not perform even these functions efficiently unless they acted together—that even their strictly internal policies were coming more and more to depend on the assurance that the policies of other governments did not conflict with them. And from 1919

8

the field in which the state could operate without taking other states into account, on the assumption that it was a separate sovereign unit, contracted at an even more rapid rate than before.

But if the League merely facilitated the extension of international co-ordination in the administration of economic, social and technical problems that were common to all states, at least it met with no serious obstacles on this side of its work. The success of the International Labour Organisation, founded in close association with the League, with the aim of improving the conditions of labour in all countries by the process of debating and adopting international conventions and recommendations, was only the most notable example of the steady if unspectacular progress that it achieved.

To a smaller extent the same was true of another field, in which the League's provisions constituted a more novel departure. The mandates system, a half-way house between the annexation of the colonies of the defeated states, which was finally avoided in 1919, and the internationalisation of all the world's undeveloped areas, which was not practicable, made the mandatory states answerable to a permanent Commission of the League for the administration of their mandate territories. Though the system was applied only to territories taken from the defeated—to Germany's colonies and to the Arab territories of the Ottoman Empire—and though the answerability turned out in practice to be little more than a formality, this Commission did preserve and develop the principle of international accountability for dependent territories until it was more firmly established in the trusteeship system of the United Nations.

It was otherwise with the central problems which inspired the foundation of the League. To deal with these problems at all the League had to embody a still more radical departure from previous practice and ideas. If it was to be, or to inaugurate, an international system that, unlike all its predecessors, would be effective in maintaining peace between the states, it had to introduce new rules of law into their political relations, that area where the only rule of law as yet had been the unlimited right of every state to go to war. It had also to ensure, however, that these rules would be enforced against potential law-breakers, who themselves would be states. Hence the inescapable dilemma that, while the objective was to avoid the use of force, the use of force might be the ultimate resort.

This dilemma dictated the early collapse of the League. It also dictated the drafting of the League's Covenant. This incorporated different approaches to the problem which the pressure of circumstances and their own aspirations set for the men who drew it up. It was because they recognised the dilemma, but sought to escape it, that, although these approaches were distinct and overlapping, rather than diametrically in conflict, they did not properly reconcile them even in this document or constitution with which the League was launched.

The first approach built on existing, if recent, developments relating to the peaceful settlement of interstate disputes. During the nineteenth century the critics of the international system had increasingly come to believe that the system would be improved only if it was made compulsory for states to submit all their disputes to the judicial process of arbitration—that it would, indeed, be perfected if this could be achieved. From the beginning of the twentieth century this view had begun to give way to the realisation that, since in most international disputes of any importance at least one of the parties seeks not its legal right but a change in the existing political situation, the chief defect of the international system was rather the lack of a reliable political procedure for the settlement of quarrels without the resort to war. Furthermore, governments themselves had begun to recognise the seriousness of this defect. At the Hague Conferences of 1899 and 1907 they had, it is true, at last set up the International Court of Arbitration. But they had also repeated that it was in their view desirable that states should offer their mediation or good offices to assist disputing states to agree upon a settlement, and, more than that, they had introduced the novel conciliation procedure by which *ad hoc* Commissions of Enquiry might be set up to report on the facts of a dispute. By 1914 another extension of conciliation procedure had been brought in by the first of the Bryan treaties in which, if only bilaterally, Great Britain and the United States agreed to refer all disputes "of every nature whatsoever" to a Standing Peace Commission for report. In that part of it which emphasised the peaceful settlement of disputes (Articles 12–17) the Covenant of the League went further in this direction in three ways.

While it recognised that only a limited number of disputes were amenable to arbitration, and that there was thus little point in making arbitration compulsory, it bound the member states of the League to submit their disputes either to arbitration or to the process of enquiry and report by the League's Council. In the second place, it created for the member states the further express obligation to refrain from war during a "moratorium" in which either arbitration or the conciliation efforts of the Council were given the opportunity to work. Finally, in the attempt to ensure that these obligations would be carried out, it laid it down that should any member state go to war in disregard of them—or go to war against another which had abided by them—it should *ipso facto* be deemed to have committed an act of war against all the other members, which would at once subject its nationals to the severance of all commercial, financial and personal intercourse with all other states. In Article 17 it extended the same sanction against a non-member state which went to war with a member state after either disregarding the League's arbitration and conciliation procedures or refusing to be bound by them.

By obliging states to employ procedures for the pacific settlement of their disputes, and not to resort to war without exhausting them, and by empowering an organisation of the states to pass judgment on the observation of these obligations and to apply sanctions if they were violated, these provisions constituted a radical new departure. To say that they altered the foundation of international law is to underestimate them. They instituted—at least they sought to do so—an international law in that area where none had previously existed and where alone a truly international or public law could subsist—the political relations between states. At the same time, however, they recognised that this law would be subject to limitations in its operation, in that they did not seek either to abolish the right of the state to go to war or to impose on the state the duty of resorting to war against law-breaking states.

In relation to the right to war they drew a firm distinction between the obligation to comply with their peace-seeking procedures and, on the other hand, the obligation to accept whatever settlement of a dispute might be recommended as a result of doing so. In the event of a dispute being submitted to the Council, they empowered the Council only to recommend a settlement, not to impose one, if it failed to persuade the parties to agree. If the Council's recommendation (disputants excepted) was not unanimous, the parties were free to go to war after the expiry of the moratorium. In such a situation the other states were also to be quite free: they reserved to themselves the right to take such action "for right and justice" as they considered necessary. In the same way, the Council could only propose what steps they should take if, having agreed to accept arbitration, a state failed to comply with an arbitration award.

Where the provisions committed the member states to take action—that is, when a state went to war without submitting a dispute to arbitration or to the Council, or before the moratorium had expired, or against another state which had accepted an arbitration award or a settlement unanimously recommended by the Council—they incorporated a different limitation. Here they drew an equally sharp distinction between the application of the economic sanction, which was to be automatic, and the resort to war. Over and above the economic sanction, Article 16 of the Covenant did envisage the need to resort to war "to protect the Covenants of the League". But it empowered the Council only to recommend what military forces the members should contribute if this need arose. As to when it might arise, it was totally obscure.

From what has been said—not to speak of all we know about the preparation and drafting of this part of the Covenant, which was largely the work of British international lawyers and Foreign Office officials—it may be deduced that of all the considerations underlying these articles the most prominent was the assumption, or at least the hope, that war would be avoidable if the resort to it could be postponed until the facts in a dispute had been sifted and published. This assumption had already inspired the pre-war innovations in conciliation procedure, and it had been reinforced in many minds by reflection on the circumstances in which war had broken out in 1914. On the other hand, another assumption was no less powerful: the assumption that, while states might adjust so far as to accept a radical extension of conciliation procedure, they were unlikely to do so to the extent of binding themselves to accept, or of accepting in fact, such settlements as were proposed as a result of this procedure. In any serious dispute, at least the great states would be inclined to insist, rather, on the resort to war if the outcome failed to satisfy them. And since this was so — and British officials knew that it was so for Great Britain — a final consideration came into play.

If it was unwise — indeed, incompatible with the hope that was being placed in the procedures aimed at postponing war — to attempt to impose settlements on states, it was no less important to avoid committing all states to resort to war whenever one of their number did so. Their right to abstain from war except in pursuit of their own best judgment was as much to be respected as their right to go to war, if only in the last resort, in pursuit of their interests or security.

Despite their cautiousness, these calculations would have produced a radical change. Theoretically, a League based on them would have permitted a state to evade the "peaceful settlement" provisions. By abiding by them until the moratorium had lapsed, and then declaring war, it could still have gone to war quite legally. In the other direction — by leaving each member state to decide for itself whether the occasion for the automatic sanction had arisen; by permitting the Council only to recommend more drastic action, and only to recommend settlements; by applying to the deliberations of the Council the rule by which member states retained their freedom unless its recommendations were unanimous — it would theoretically have permitted a state to evade its obligation to act against breaches of those provisions. In fact, although they did not call for the complete renunciation of war, they made it highly improbable that an aggressor state could resort to war without violating its covenants; and none of the wars which occurred while the League existed began in this way. All of them either involved breaches of a state's obligation to resort to peaceful settlement, or would have done so if the state had been a member of the League. In the same way, while these provisions left it possible for states to evade their obligation to apply sanctions against such breaches, they did not permit them to do so honestly: the occasion for the sanction was very precisely defined.

But it was not after a dispassionate examination of their probable consequences that they were judged to be inadequate. When Wilson, the President of the United States, decided that they yielded a League that "lacked teeth", he did so in the conviction that they were too conservative. The peace settlement made possible, and experience demanded, a still more radical departure from previous practices and ways.

This conviction, the origin of the second element that is to be found in the Covenant, was widely shared by 1919. But for the fact that the United States government embraced it, however, it is unlikely that the victor states would have been swayed by it. It was President Wilson who determined that the League should be set up as something more than a peaceful procedure device — as what he called "a community of power" — on the basis of what came to be termed "collective security".

As interpreted by him — and he interpreted it accurately enough — the conviction envisaged the purpose of an international organisation as being to preserve "the new order" which the peace-settlement was about to establish. It would do this only if it substituted international for national interests, open discussion for secret diplomacy, joint action against aggression for the outmoded alliance and the discredited balance of power.

The first outcome of this programme was his insistence that the Covenant of the League must incorporate the provision (Article 10) by which each member state undertook to preserve as against external aggression the territorial integrity and political independence of every member state. Its second outcome was his failure to include in the Covenant any precise procedure for activating this guarantee or for obtaining the common action that its implementation would entail. If it was essential to outlaw aggression against an enlightened and democratically inspired peace-settlement, it was also unnecessary to provide for action against aggression within a League made up, as he wished it to be, only of democratically self-governing states. Within and against such a League, given that it would have its peaceful settlement procedures for investigating and reporting the facts of a dispute, the force of public opinion would itself be sufficient to ensure that aggression would not take place. Indeed, he did not merely omit to make any provisions which went beyond these procedures, but also thwarted a French attempt to do so.

The French government, which strongly supported the inclusion of Article 10, demanded that the Covenant should also lay down a precise procedure for collective security against aggression. It wished to establish an international police force under the League, or at least an international General Staff to advise the League's Council when and how to apply military sanctions against Covenant breakers. Wilson objected to any such step as being calculated to convert the League into just that kind of military alliance which would be incompatible with the new spirit he hoped to inaugurate. France succeeded in obtaining only Article 9 of the Covenant, which created a commission to advise the Council generally on military questions. In her opposition to Wilson's insistence on including Article 8 she failed completely. This declared that peace required the reduction of national armaments, charged the League's Council with the task of formulating plans for the reduction, and laid it down that, once the reduction had been achieved, armaments were to be increased only with the Council's consent.

In his opposition to the French demands, as in his insistence on Article 8, the President was supported by the British government. Unlike the French, who equated the mutual guarantee of Article 10 with the maintenance of the peace-settlement and wanted the League to be the military enforcement machinery for both, the British hoped to use the League as a means of conciliating or appeasing the ex-enemy states. By the same token, however, they were fundamentally opposed both to Wilson's wish to limit membership of the League to democratic self-governing states, which they persuaded him to abandon, and also to his Article 10. As well as feeling, with the French, that this would commit the League to enforcing the 1919 peace treaties, which were beginning to assume a harsh aspect in British eyes, they feared that it would burden the British government with onerous obligations which would clash with its attachment to disarmament. Quite apart from these immediate considerations, moreover, they judged that it was unwise to underwrite the *status quo* with so blanket a guarantee at a time when economic and other changes were sure to demand and to justify its revision.

In the end, the British government was so anxious that a League should be launched, though far from confident that it would succeed in transforming the international system, and so anxious to bind the United States into this system, though beginning to question whether this would prove possible, that it yielded to the President's insistence on the principle of collective security. At the same time, it succeeded in incorporating into the Covenant an article (Article 19) empowering the Assembly of the League to recommend to member states the reconsideration of treaties which had become inapplicable and also the revision of conditions which might endanger the peace of the world. In Article 11, again, it somewhat offset the rigidity of the collective guarantee.

This article enunciated Wilson's basic point: "any war or threat of war, whether immediately affecting any of the Members of the League or not", was declared to be "a matter of concern to the whole League". But it also declared it to be "the friendly right of each Member of the League to bring to the attention of the Assembly or the Council any circumstance whatever . . . which threatens to disturb international peace or the good understanding between nations upon which peace depends". And it provided that in any such emergency the Council of the League should "take any action that may be deemed wise and effectual to safeguard the peace of nations".

As finally drafted, therefore, and in the form in which it came into force, the Covenant was an uneasy combination. On the one

hand, a precise procedure for the peaceful settlement of international disputes visited breaches of the procedure with sanctions
short of war, but gave no absolute guarantee either that war
would be avoided or that it would be resorted to against states
which embarked on it. On the other hand, an absolute collective
territorial guarantee against aggression lacked a precise procedure for enforcing it. Furthermore, while such vague references
as were made to the sanction of war against breaches of this
guarantee were undermined by the emphasis given elsewhere in
the Covenant to the reconsideration of treaties and the revision
of the *status quo*, the provision made for this reconsideration was
weakened by the separate existence of the guarantee itself.

In the last resort, the differences of view which resulted in these
gaps in the Covenant mirrored those which had plagued relations
between the European states during and after the peace-settlement
of 1815, when they were embarking upon the modern international
system.

In President Wilson's vision of a League of democratic self-
governing states, dedicated to his proposition that "nobody can
hereafter be neutral as respect the disturbance of the world's peace
for an object which the world's opinion cannot sanction", it is not
fanciful to see the reflection of the Holy Alliance by which, as the
Tsar had then hoped, the Christian sovereigns of Europe would
conduct international affairs "as members of one and the same
Christian nation". The French government's support of Wilson's
League, in the less visionary hope of converting it into a machine
for upholding and enforcing the new peace-settlement, recalls the
policy of Metternich, the Austrian Chancellor—a policy which
had combined contempt for the principles of the Holy Alliance
with the determination to divert it to the cause of suppressing
revolution and maintaining an equilibrium in the interest of
autocracy. Great Britain's advocacy against the American and the
French positions of the principles of the peaceful settlement of
disputes and peaceful change to the *status quo* closely resembled
the insistence of Castlereagh, her Foreign Secretary at that earlier
time, as against the attitudes of the Tsar and the Chancellor, that

the Congress system must be kept distinct from the Holy Alliance and be developed as a strictly diplomatic device to assist the great states to solve strictly diplomatic problems by compromise.

For some years after 1815 the aims of the Holy Alliance had dominated the early development of the Congress system. In much the same way, again, the early years of the League's existence witnessed a powerful movement to close those gaps in the Covenant which had made it something less than the League as the more radical section of the Peace Movement headed by Wilson had envisaged it, and than French interests required. Its aims were to make recourse to arbitration compulsory in all international disputes; to make it impossible for a state legally to resort to war if, after a dispute had been submitted to the League for inquiry and report, the League failed to reach a unanimous recommendation; to "put teeth into" the League's collective territorial guarantee by devising a precise definition of aggression and instituting firmer and more precise commitments to the *status quo*. This was the burden of the Draft Treaty of Mutual Assistance of 1923–4, of the Geneva Protocol to the Covenant of 1925, of a Resolution of the Assembly of the League in 1927. But by the last of these dates it was so obvious that these aims could not be realised by revision of the Covenant that the movement had already gone outside the League for the negotiation of the Pact of Paris (or Briand-Kellogg Pact) of 1928. This sought to accomplish them by declaring that the states which signed it would never solve international disputes, of whatever nature or origin, except by pacific means, and that, on behalf of their peoples, they condemned and renounced war as an instrument of national policy except in self-defence or as a sanction for the violation of the Pact.

As it was concluded outside the League, the Pact of Paris, the first attempt to declare unequivocally that aggressive war was an international crime, survived the League. By the end of the Second World War, indeed, when this principle was reaffirmed by the Nuremburg and Tokyo War Crimes Tribunals and by unanimous resolution of the first General Assembly of the United Nations, it had become accepted as part of general international law, thus completing the first fundamental change in the history of international law in regard to the legality of war. But during the remaining years of the League's existence the Pact did nothing to delay the League's collapse. When the Holy Alliance version of the Congress system was abandoned, in the early years of the modern international system, the leading states of the time fell back upon the alternative of operating the Concert of Europe as a means of securing compromise among themselves. In the 1920s, when the effort to "put teeth into" the League as an instrument of collective security was abandoned, the possibility that the League of Nations could be developed on the different lines laid down in other parts of the Covenant—as a means of promoting peaceful settlement and peaceful change—was also declining fast.

Long before the attempt to "put teeth into" the League had come to nothing—or to nothing more substantial than the Pact of Paris—member states had become restive about such obligations as it had imposed on them. They had little success in formally abolishing the most onerous—that by which under Article 10 they had undertaken to respect and preserve against external aggression the territorial integrity and political independence of all other members when advised to do so by the Council—though Canada moved its suppression at the first League Assembly in 1920. Since the Article did not make it clear whether or not the Council's advice was binding, Canada tried in 1923 to establish at least that it was purely optional. She failed by one vote, with half of the members abstaining. It was never settled, however, whether, in giving its advice, the Council must be unanimous, or unanimous except for the votes of the interested parties, or might act by majority vote: though frequently appealed to, Article 10 was never applied. Nor was this because the member states preferred to operate the sanction to which they were committed by the peaceful settlement Articles of the Covenant. They were no less anxious to evade this, and they were more successful in doing so.

At the first League Assembly the Scandinavian members proposed amendments which would have authorised the Council to exempt states from the application of the automatic sanction of Article 16. Their proposals failed; but the second Assembly in 1921 adopted resolutions by which the League agreed not only that it was the duty of each member state to decide for itself whether a breach of the peaceful settlement procedure had been committed, but also that a state of war did not automatically follow upon an act of war. The existence of a state of war between two countries depended upon their intentions, not upon their acts. On the only occasion on which Article 16 was invoked, against Italy's attack on Abyssinia in 1935, the member states used these resolutions in order to avoid imposing the automatic and total economic sanctions which the Article required from them. As was said at that time, the resolutions had been adopted because a literal interpretation of Article 16 "would lead to results so extravagant and so obviously contrary to the spirit of the Covenant that it has been recognised that they must be interpreted with some degree of latitude, though in this case the word 'interpretation' is something of a euphemism".[1]

We cannot be surprised by this development at a time when the overriding wish of many states was the avoidance of war, when the obligation to impose sanctions was associated with the maintenance of a *status quo* with which many states felt little sympathy, and when the resort to sanctions might lead to attack by the state against whom they were invoked in a fundamentally unstable situation. One reason for the bleakness of the League's experience in the 1920s and the 1930s, indeed, as compared with the revival of the Concert experiment a hundred years before, after it had all but foundered, is to be found in the difference between international conditions at the two periods. The Congress or Concert experiment had been undertaken at a time when, for all the divergences of opinion and of development between the states of Europe, there was fundamental agreement on the wisdom of upholding the peace settlement of 1815 and a fundamental stability, which the peace settlement had reinforced, in terms of the relative power of the leading states. When the League was launched, a massive shift in the distribution of international power, at work since the 1870s, was still in train, and an unusually unstable phase in the development of the weapons and techniques of war, which had set in from the same time, was still in full

[1] Brierly, J. L. (2nd edn, 1936), *The Law of Nations*, p. 243.

transition. More than that, the efforts demanded by the First World War and the dramatic character of its results had compounded the instability.

By overthrowing regimes and dislocating societies, by ensuring after years of popular enthusiasm for blood-letting and months of weariness with war that the punishment of the enemy would be the central object in any peace treaty, and by accelerating technical change, the war determined that a new peace settlement would have to be made at just the point in a period of great transition when instability was at its height. Being made at such a time, it not only lacked the collaboration of the defeated states and of a Russia that was in full revolution, but also quickly lost the adhesion of the extra-European victor powers. In the years before 1914 the incorporation of these states in the international system, and particularly of the United States and Japan, had begun to loom large as one of the requirements of its ability to adjust and survive. In the years after 1919, after a brief participation in the system at a time of crisis, these states lapsed into an isolationism that was more profound than before at a time when the system's ability to recover was even more dependent on their willingness to adhere to it.

The 1919 settlement was bound in these circumstances to fail to fulfil the longing for a return to stable times. It was not only the case, however, that international conditions permitted no early return to stability. In the aftermath of the First World War the requirements of a stable international system had come to include, alongside the conciliation of defeated or shattered powers and the incorporation of more of the world's states, the achievement of a far greater change in the behaviour and attitudes of states than the Concert system had called for. That system had been made possible by the fact that the leading states had come to accept, by the beginning of the nineteenth century, that they were members of an international system who must work together as far as possible if the system was to serve their increasingly complex interests. Though its effectiveness had been prolonged to the end of that century by their increasing reluctance to fight each other, it had not involved their abandonment of the right to establish the legal condition of belligerency by resorting to war. By 1919 it seemed plain to all who hoped to safeguard the international system against total collapse that, as the wisdom of the reluctance to embark on war had been amply confirmed, so the limitation or the abolition of the right to do so had become the next essential step. But it was to be less easy for states to bring this about than it had been, earlier, for them to recognise the need to collaborate as states.

In the unstable circumstances in which this step was attempted, the immediate effects of the necessarily ambitious programme that resulted from it were even more unfortunate. If only because it lacked the membership of the United States and Russia from the outset, of Japan after 1931, of Italy after 1937, of Germany except between 1926 and 1933, the League of Nations could not fill the immense gap between the reality of international disorder and the desire for international progress except by encouraging dangerous illusions. But it would be to perpetuate some of these illusions to stress that the League was launched at an unpropitious time, without also insisting that it was also naive in the expectations on which it was founded.

Until states had discovered and developed still more powerful deterrents against the resort to war they could not escape, and they could not solve, a conflict which these expectations had over-looked — the conflict between their reluctance to engage in war and the need to rely on it as the means of upholding not only their own interests, but also the stability of the international system. When they had discovered and developed these still more powerful deterrents, after a second World War and a fearful expansion in the scale of force at their disposal, they also discovered in their even greater concern to avoid war that they could avoid this same conflict only by lowering their earlier expectations.

At the end of the Second World War, in the rules it laid down for governing the resort to war by the individual state, the Charter of the United Nations Organisation took over from the League the principles of peaceful settlement and collective security. Member states were bound to settle their disputes by peaceful means in such a way that international peace, security and justice were not endangered (Article 2(3)), and to refer these disputes to the Security Council if they failed to settle them by negotiation or other pacific means (Articles 33 and 37). They were bound to refrain in their international relations from the threat or use of force against the territorial integrity or political independence of any state, or in any other manner inconsistent with the purposes of the United Nations (Article 2(4)). Except in self-defence or in the execution of collective measures authorised by the United Nations in the common interest, the use or threat of armed force was thus prohibited. In one direction, moreover, the Charter was far stricter than the Covenant in the provisions it made for ensuring that these obligations would be observed—or that breaches of them would be punished.

The League had permitted member states to decide for themselves whether the obligation to observe its peace-settlement procedure had been neglected; and in the case of military action being called for against breaches of it, their independence had been further safeguarded by obscurity as to whether the Council's recommendations were to be binding. In the event of breaches of the collective territorial guarantee in Article 10, the Council's recommendations had been binding, at least if they were unanimous, but member states had remained free to decide what action they would take to give effect to them. The United Nations Organisation deprived member states of these safeguards. Whereas the Covenant had sought to solve the problem of subjecting the use of force to law by relying on the fulfilment of undertakings—which the member states had severally given—to take prescribed measures against a state which violated them, the Charter constituted for the first time a supra-national authority for this purpose.

It did so by giving the Security Council the power not merely to co-ordinate the actions of its members, but also to issue directions to them as to what these actions should be, against any threat to peace or breach of the peace or act of aggression (Articles 40–49). The Security Council's decisions were made binding on member states, who agreed "to accept and carry out the decisions of the Security Council" (Article 25). It laid down, further, that the Organisation should ensure that non-member states acted in accordance with its principles (Article 2). Nor did it overlook that in a situation in which, except in self-defence, war had ceased to be a legal category and all use of force had been designated as an international crime, states would be tempted to portray and justify acts of aggression as acts of self-defence, even as War Offices were to be renamed Ministries of Defence and general staffs were to be merged into National Security Councils. Although the Charter reserved individual and collective self-defence as an inherent right of states, it subjected this right to the judgment and control of the Security Council by insisting that the Security Council should be advised of all measures taken under this head, and that its own authority to act should remain unaffected (Article 51).

It was "in order to ensure prompt and effective action" that the Security Council was thus given the "primary responsibility for the maintenance of international peace and security", and that member states agreed that "in carrying out its duties under this responsibility the Security Council acts on their behalf" (Article 24). In the same cause the Charter abandoned the League's attachment to the principle of unanimity in the making of decisions. The Security Council might act by an affirmative vote of seven of its eleven members. In another direction however — in relation to the powers of the Security Council, as opposed to the obligations of the individual member states — the Charter embodied a quite different logic from that which had characterised the Covenant. The League had been designed to uphold legality always, and peace as far as possible. The activation of its members' obligations had depended on the violation of precise covenants, or procedures, for peaceful settlement and of an absolute territorial guarantee, and it had ultimately involved the preparedness of members to go to war against offenders. Although "justice" was referred to in its preamble and in Article 2(3) of the Charter, the United Nations Organisation was less interested in just or legal settlement of disputes than in the avoidance of war.

9

Its central thesis was that any settlement was better than war. Accordingly, the Charter clearly distinguished between the powers of the Security Council in relation to the promotion of the peaceful settlement of disputes and its powers in relation to the resort to enforcement-action in the event that peaceful settlement failed. As it enjoined member states to seek the peaceful settlement of their disputes, by whatever means appealed to them (Article 33), so it gave the Security Council little power in that field: the Council could investigate a dispute and recommend a settlement, but its recommendations could be recommendations only (Article 31). But it was otherwise in the matter of deciding whether and, if so, what action was required to prevent a dispute from disturbing the peace. The Covenant had laid down precise tests for deciding whether the occasion for sanctions had arisen. The Charter left it entirely to the Security Council to decide whether a threat to peace or a breach of covenant or an act of aggression had arisen, and what action should be taken "to maintain or restore international peace and security" (Article 39). It was free to decide that no occasion for action had arisen. In reaching its decisions there was nothing, apart from its general obligation to act in accordance with the purposes and principles of the Charter, to ensure that it paid regard to the legality or illegality of the actions of the states involved. In proportion as the United Nations Organisation was made freer than the League to take effective action, by inroads into the freedom of its members to abstain from action and by a less legalistic conception of the occasions on which action would be required, its action was subjected to the discretion of its executive body, and that discretion was made a matter of political decision. In all the Articles which dealt with its peace-keeping functions, the powers of the Security Council were permissive as well as complete.

This change involved a further limitation on the freedom of the individual member state—a limitation, this time, on its freedom to initiate action. In the Covenant, Article 11 had enabled any member of the League to summon a meeting of the Council to discuss a threat to peace. By Article 15 any member had been free to decide that there had been a violation of the peaceful-settlement procedure. In the Charter the member states lost these discretions no less than their freedom not to act if called upon by the Security Council to do so. A similar change of emphasis was made when the Charter redrafted the League's collective guarantee of the territorial integrity and political independence of every member state. The Charter in Article 2(4) repeated the obligation of each member to respect these things and to refrain from the threat or use of force against them. It did not guarantee that the Security Council would preserve them and, with them, the *status quo*. An absolute guarantee of each by all was replaced by a conditional guarantee of all by the Security Council.

In sharp contrast both to its concern for effectiveness in action and to its avoidance of any commitment to the *status quo*, the Charter diverged from the Covenant in yet another way. It specified by name (Article 23) the five Great Powers to which it allotted permanent seats on the Security Council and to which it granted the individual right to veto action by the Security Council. If the work of the United Nations was subjected to the power of the Security Council in the interests of effective action, the power of the Security Council was subjected to the discretion of each of its Great Power members in that its decisions required the affirmative votes of seven members and that these seven votes had to include the concurring votes of all five permnaent members.

Two views have been expressed about the veto provisions of the Charter. Some have maintained that the move from the Covenant to the Charter was, in view of these provisions, "to exchange a system which might or might not have worked for one which cannot work, and that instead of limiting the sovereignty of states we have actually extended the sovereignty of the Great Powers, the only states whose sovereignty is still a formidable reality in the modern world."[1] The other view has

[1] Brierly, J. L. (1946), "The Covenant and the Charter" in *British Yearbook of International Law*. See also Brierly, J. L. (6th edn, 1963), *The Law of Nations*, p. 385.

held that the drafters of the Charter were being realistic when they recognised, reluctantly or otherwise, that, precisely because the sovereignty of the Great Powers was a reality, the United Nations Organisation could be effective only if the Great Powers were disposed to work together. Even though it had no veto, the League of Nations would still have been inoperable against a Great Power, without a major war. Was it not among the lessons to be learned from the League's collapse that, by allowing the veto, the Charter might assist them to co-operate in avoiding war, which was what it was designed to achieve?

Whichever of these views we adopt, there can be no disagreement on two points of historical fact. The arrangements initially made in the Charter for limiting the operation of the veto have proved ineffectual. All attempts to evade its operation by amending the Charter or ignoring its provisions have also failed.

In the Charter the veto does not apply to decisions on procedure (which may be made by the votes of any seven members of the Security Council), or when a member is party to a dispute which the Security Council is investigating; in this case that member must abstain. It has turned out, however, that, as the question whether a particular matter is or is not procedural is not itself a question of procedure, the permanent members can use the veto on that preliminary question. Nor is that all. Since the Charter distinguishes between a dispute and "a situation which might . . . give rise to a dispute", the question whether there is or is not a dispute is also one on which the veto can be used. In practice the veto power of the permanent members has been complete, as the Soviet government originally demanded that it should be.

The veto provisions of the Charter were a compromise between the Soviet position and that of the British government. The latter sought to deny to the Great Powers the right to veto either the peaceful-settlement recommendations or the enforcement measures of the Security Council in disputes to which they were parties. It may safely be asserted that none of the permanent members would now wish to revive the British view or to limit in other ways their veto power. For some years after the Charter was signed, however, determined attempts were made to evade the operation of the veto either by amending the Charter or by circumventing its main provisions.

The first occurred during the Korean War. On account of the temporary withdrawal of the Soviet delegate, the Security Council was able in June 1950 to determine the existence of an armed attack by North Korea upon South Korea, to call for the withdrawal of North Korean forces and to recommend members of the United Nations Organisation to assist South Korea by pooling their forces under a United Nations Command. The return of the Soviet Union to the Security Council, and the fear that it would use the veto to suspend or impede this exercise in collective security, led to the adoption in November 1950 by the General Assembly of the "Uniting for Peace" Resolution. This arranged that, when the Security Council was prevented from discharging its responsibility for maintaining peace by a Great Power's use of its veto, the matter might be transferred to the General Assembly, which might recommend to the parties to a dispute measures for bringing it to an end and, if necessary, recommend to the member states collective enforcement-measures for the purpose of restoring or maintaining peace. To ensure that these measures would be effective it also established a permanent Peace Observation Committee of fourteen members, which could visit and report on dangerous situations, and a permanent Collective Measures Committee of fourteen members to study the methods to be employed for maintaining the peace.

As a result of this resolution, which effected a virtual amendment of the Charter, the General Assembly acquired a voice in the executive zone of the United Nations Organisation which it has not since lost. But the enlargement of its voice was not accompanied by an enlargement of its powers; unlike the Security Council, it could only recommend action to the member states. Partly on this account, and partly because it proved difficult to pass recommendations requiring two thirds of the votes in an Assembly that was designed as a legislature and that was steadily increasing in size, the only lasting effect of the resolution has been to make it possible for the Assembly to be convened for the discussion of emergencies. When it has succeeded in resolving to call for action, its recommendations have either been responded to with great caution or not heeded at all by member states. Its Peace Observation Committee has been used only once—it studied the situation on Greece's borders with Albania and Bulgaria in 1951–2. After making annual reports on general problems between 1951 and 1954, its Collective Measures Committee also retreated into inactivity.

There followed a brief period in which the General Assembly (acting under the "Uniting for Peace" Resolution) and the Security Council attempted to devolve the execution of their responsibilities upon the Secretary-General of the UN. The first result of this, the second course adopted in the hope of circumventing the veto, was the establishment by the Secretary-General in 1956 of a United Nations Force in Egypt to secure and supervise, on behalf of the General Assembly, the cessation of hostilities after the Suez Crisis. The last of any consequence occurred in 1960. In that year, authorised by the Council and the Assembly to provide the government of the Congo with military assistance until it was able to meet its own responsibilities, the Secretary-General took charge of the formation of a United Nations Congo Force, its dispatch to the Congo, the appointment of its Chief of Command, and its employment there, in consultation with the government, as a military extension of the Secretariat itself.

It was not solely because the government of the Congo disintegrated, following the Council's call for the withdrawal of Belgian troops, that this undertaking quickly turned into a fiasco. It was not solely because the fiasco brought the United Nations to financial bankruptcy that it is unlikely to be repeated. Apart from its repetition on a small scale in Cyprus, the Congo operation has proved to be the last attempt by the Secretary-General to restore or maintain peace in a difficult area by introducing a United Nations Force, when the Security Council can agree only on generalities—as the Korean War has proved to be the last attempt to use the United Nations Organisation for enforcement action in a dispute on which the Security Council cannot agree at all—for more substantial reasons. In the first place, the Secretariat is no more fitted to deal with political crises, as opposed to supervising international administrative organisations, than is the General Assembly. The Civil Service of the United Nations Organisation, as the General Assembly is its legislature, it necessarily brought the attitudes of the administrator, and particularly the false conviction that political problems are administratively soluble, to the unexpected extension of its functions into the political field. It was for this reason that it underestimated the complexity of the burdens it assumed, and failed to anticipate that by assuming them it would incur obstruction and criticism from Great Powers which insisted that it was exceeding its powers and usurping their rights.

This criticism combined with the setback in the Congo to bring about the abandonment by the Secretary-General of the political initiative and the executive responsibility he had so recently begun to assume. At one level it constituted yet another source of contention between the Great Powers, being voiced by Soviet Russia and France and rebutted by the United States and the United Kingdom. In reality, however, a second reason for the Secretary-General's retreat to his original limited functions was the fact that tension between the Great Powers was at last beginning to decline. Like the attempt to circumvent the veto by giving the General Assembly an executive role in the implementation of the Charter, his assumption of a wider role had been a reflection of the total distrust which had prevailed between the Western Powers and Soviet Russia during the worst years of the Cold War. With the onset, from the early 1960s, of direct, if still tentative, diplomatic understanding and political adjustment between the two Great Power blocs, interest in continuing either of these experiments would still have waned even if experience had not shown that they could not make the United Nations Organisation effective in the absence of co-operation between the Great Powers.

With the decline of tension between the Great Powers, indeed, if not as yet the rise of constructive co-operation between them, a further development took place: the decline of interest in the United Nations Organisation even as an instrument of Great Power co-operation. During the worst of the Cold War, Russia relied on her veto to protect her interests and used the United Nations Organisation as an arena for ideological recrimination. Other states did not resist the urge to free the United Nations Organisation from the Russian veto and to use it as an ideological façade for the pursuit of their own interests. The "Uniting for Peace" Resolution and the support given to the political initiative of the Secretary-General arose at least in part from this motive. But these manoeuvres, and particularly the second of them, were also inspired by a more elevated consideration: many genuinely resisted the thought that the United Nations Organisation might be reduced to being a tool of the Great Powers or an entirely optional accessory to their diplomacy in consequence of the veto provisions. And as well as terminating the effort of the Great Powers to turn the United Nations against each other, their return to diplomacy dissipated the more idealistic support for the United Nations Organisation by revealing that it cannot avoid this fate.

While the Great Powers were at loggerheads it was either inoperable or it was misused. If they continue to co-operate — if they at last come to terms with the need to replace the modern international system with one which reflects their experience and responds to the vast changes that are taking place in international conditions — it will either be ignored, as being unnecessary, or it will prove to be a useful channel for their co-operation and perhaps even a moral check on their conduct; and it can avoid being ignored only if it obtains interest in and support for its performance of these secondary roles.

PART III : CONCLUSION

CHAPTER NINE

Nationalism and the International System in the Second Half of the Twentieth Century

During the first fifty years of the modern international system, from the 1820s to the 1870s, its states retained the right to go to war for any reason whatever, indeed for no reason at all, but they subscribed to the doctrine of equilibrium—to the principle of the balance of power in its modern sense—out of their concern to establish more stable international relations. Between the 1870s and the beginning of the twentieth century, when an actual equilibrium between them was passing away, the need to preserve or restore it became their main justification of the right to war, which remained the only fundamental principle of international law. During the next fifty years the aim in all their efforts to establish a stable international system was to restrict the right to war of every state by instituting between all states a public law, of which the fundamental principles were the peaceful settlement of disputes and collective security.

Since the end of the Second World War this aim has in some sense been achieved: the majority of states have at last accepted it to be part of general international law that, except in self-defence or in the exercise of their obligation to uphold the principles of peaceful settlement and collective security, the resort to force in international relations is illegal, not to say a crime. But it has been achieved at the expense of widespread disenchantment with the results.

The disenchantment has taken two forms. In one of them the aim is judged to have been right but it is conceded that the pursuit of it has been premature. This is particularly the view of international lawyers. Though some of them still hail the development of international law as a great advance, and still confidently expect it to yield other advances, their severest critics are other international lawyers who admit or insist that the development has been accomplished within a political or constitutional international framework which has prevented it from effecting any substantial change in the character of international relations. The veto provisions of the UN Charter, the keystone of this framework, were the price which the United Nations Organisation had to pay for creating, in the shape of the Security Council, an organ invested with the power to act and decide in a corporate capacity within a loose and at best a confederal society of independent states. The decision to establish such an organ in such a society inevitably produced the veto, and thus a Security Council that can seldom act or decide. It was no more possible to change the character of this society by endowing it with an institution appropriate to a more advanced type of society than it is to turn a nation into a democracy by giving it a democratic constitution.

> International institutions cannot be raised from the co-operative to the organic level until we have a society of states which is far more closely bound together than are the states of today, until, in short, nations have the same sort of confidence in one another's intentions and policies and the same absence of fundamental diversity of interests that the states of a federation must have if their union is to endure.[1]

These arguments are common to most legal critics of the United Nations, who differ only in their assessment of the prospects of achieving a virtually federal relationship between states.

Some of these critics, perhaps the majority, are silent on this point, confining themselves to the argument that the veto is an understandable as well as an inevitable consequence until such a relationship has developed. Others are emphatic that it is

[1] Brierly, J. L. (6th edn, 1963), *The Law of Nations*, p. 113.

utopian to expect such a relationship to evolve among the states of today. To suppose that these states could agree to establish a federal world state is to overlook "all the social forces which support . . . the contemporary international system of power politics in disguise". The same objection applies to the argument that they will unwittingly become so integrated as to constitute a federal state, as a result of the gradual evolution of existing international law and political institutions or of the development of functional co-operation in technical and non-political fields. There is no warrant whatever for assuming that, "like the State in the classless society of Karl Marx, national sovereignty will simply wither away."[1] On the contrary, the history of the United Nations Organisation has already destroyed the possibility of believing in a gradualist solution.

Before 1919 the international system frankly recognised the role of force, and limited the rules of international law to matters which were irrelevant to international political relations. Since 1945, even more than in the days of the League, international law has been extended to the sphere of political relations between states at the expense of instituting an international system that is a system of power politics in disguise. The United Nations Organisation, more elaborate and more nearly universally accepted than its predecessor, has not only produced a great increase in procedural and administrative activity and quasi-law of the kind that obscures the actual lack of relationship between international conduct and the principles of the public law. Because it both enshrines these principles and incorporates the veto, it permits states both to evade the principles when it suits them to do so, and to invoke them in justification of their resort to the traditional methods of power politics. All states, whatever their motives and persuasions, have responded in the same way. No significant distinction may be drawn between the action of the United States in investing its armed intervention in Korea with the authority of the United Nations—or in evading the authority of the United Nations in its armed intervention in Vietnam—and the insistence of Soviet Russia that the principles

[1] Schwarzenberger, G. (1971), *International Law and Order*, pp. 23–5.

and procedures of the United Nations did not apply to its armed interventions in Hungary and Czechoslovakia.[1]

In the light of their views it is perhaps surprising that these more severe critics of the United Nations Organisation in the end conclude that "however 'utopian' *within* the existing framework of world politics, the federal pattern appears to provide the only commensurate constructive answer to the impotence of the parochial state . . . to protect its citizens against the worst . . . risks of a divided world." "What is needed is a world public order which any of the parochial states can flout only at its own risk. Anything less may be all that is attainable, but falls sadly below the world safety minimum."[2] But in the light of this conclusion we cannot be surprised that disillusionment with the results of the United Nations experiment has taken a second form — that outside the ranks of international lawyers, belief in the possibility of ever eliminating war and international instability by the development of international law and organisation is now at a lower ebb than at any time since the beginning of this century, when governments first seriously embarked on programmes which had this aim.

If it is indeed true — as the lawyers assert[3] — that this possibility depends on the establishment of a federal world state, it is for good reasons that confidence in these programmes has so markedly declined. On the one hand, as Kant pointed out nearly two hundred years ago, "a federal state of nations contains a contradiction; many nations would in a single state constitute

---

[1] Schwarzenberger, G., op. cit., pp. 16–22.

[2] ibid., pp. 217–18.

[3] Perhaps it should be recognised that there is another school of international lawyers. These are critical of the United Nations Organisation not because it falls short of being a federal system, but because it gives too much emphasis to the maintenance of peace and too little to the maintenance of international law. But they recognise the limitations of international law by insisting that the fundamental problems in international relations — those problems which in this century men have hoped to solve by institutionalising the principles of peaceful change and collective security — cannot be solved "by institutional legal means . . . or binding decisions of a political or pseudo-juridical central authority", but will "always remain a matter of prolonged political struggle and diplomatic bargaining" in which "the only hope of a peaceful solution would seem to lie in the field of negotiation and conciliation". See Verzijl, J. W. H. (Leyden, 1968), *International Law in Historical Perspective*, Vol. 2, pp. 223, 253.

only one nation, which is contradictory since we are here considering the rights of nations towards each other so long as they constitute different states and are not joined together into one." It is still the case that the establishment of a single world state, should that be feasible, would bring the international system to an end rather than advance the solution of its problems. On the other hand, it is also still the case that we have no grounds for believing it to be feasible.

At least since the eighteenth century the growth and spread of technological and managerial capacity—in industry, commerce and finance; in transport and communications; in science; in diplomacy and war—have been exerting a powerful and an increasing influence on the character of the more advanced societies and of the relations between them, making them ever more complicated in their structure and bringing them into closer and closer contact with each other. During the twentieth century, when these processes have markedly accelerated, assumptions about their probable or inevitable political consequences have played a part in reviving and expanding an old political programme. Until the beginning of the nineteenth century the belief persisted that Europe could be made into a single political community by restoring the medieval empire which had supposedly given unity to it. Since the First World War this belief has been replaced by the hope that material pressures will facilitate the creation of a United States of Europe. But its true modern equivalent has been the conviction that, as its societies become more complicated and more interlocked, the whole world will become a single political community as a result of the fusion of its states into a single world government.

Of the two programmes, the old and the modern, we need not insist that neither will ever be realised. The revival of the old one testifies to the enormous power which managerial and technological advance now exerts in the direction of political integration. But we can say with some confidence that it will only be after much disappointment to its advocates and by the most circuitous of routes that either will be reached, if ever it is reached. The processes that have inspired them have been at work for too long to leave any doubt about the fragility of expectations which underrate, as these programmes do, the diversity of the elements that are involved in political change and that account for its immense complexity.

It is not only that political forces, the structures of the separate society and the individual state, constitute formidable obstacles to the free play of the technological and managerial processes. The political effects of the processes are themselves as indiscriminate as they are pervasive. Since the Second World War they have brought some of the advanced societies, those of western Europe, to the point of experimenting with political integration. But they have also drawn a greater number and variety of advanced societies than ever before into a single international system, and they have at last reached out beyond those societies to produce new states in the undeveloped and under-developed areas of the world. In the course of doing so they have not advanced the prospects of a trans-national fusion of all these societies and states. Those of western Europe share a common history and a common civilisation. The advanced societies of the world share at most a material, if a fairly protracted, preparation for their present condition. Those of the undeveloped world have little in common, either materially or historically, with the advanced societies – or even among themselves.

Take, again, the effect of the processes on the relations between government and society within the individual community. From the middle of the nineteenth century the increasing complexity of societies and their trend towards greater uniformity have combined with the narrowing of the physical distances between them to produce an ever-increasing number and variety of interstate unions, conventions and agreements. Since the Second World War the signs have multiplied that the exploitation of this complexity and uniformity and the further reduction of these distances are producing a situation in which the state's monopoly of control in its own society is being eroded by problems and enterprises on a trans-national scale which can no longer be contained by merely interstate arrangements. But who can doubt that the same processes have simultaneously produced in every society a vast increase in the functions and the powers of the state — a constant movement towards greater centralisation — or that for every area of competence in which the state has been losing power it has been acquiring greater influence in at least one other?

In western Europe, indeed, we can perhaps already see, in the evolution of the Common Market, the outcome that these processes, with their conflicting effects, will most probably bring about in due course in the world as a whole: not a single community with a single government, but a network of competing authorities all influencing every society. At one extreme these already embrace, so far as the Common Market is concerned, interstate organisations ranging from the loose but universal political system of the United Nations, through arrangements and alliances with external states, like the North Atlantic Treaty Organisation, to bureaucratic structures for maintaining administrative standardisation and close economic co-operation which are confined to the Common Market's member states. At the other extreme they may have to come to include state arrangements ensuring the liberties within each member state of regions and provinces with devolved powers — for, as we shall see, the state is likely to be troubled by resistance to its centralisation, and perhaps by the re-emergence of regional nationalism, in proportion as it moves towards even the partial integration of its society with others. But just as it would take a bold man to prophesy whether or when this situation will extend beyond the old cockpit of western Europe to cover the relations between all the advanced centres of power in the world, let alone to incorporate those other societies which have scarcely begun upon a course which western Europe has pursued for at least two hundred years, so it would be rash to conclude that the independent territorial state will have no place in it.

The independent state is not becoming obsolete or impotent. Even in western Europe it is expanding its functions in some directions to offset their erosion in others. Beyond western Europe more states than one have attained to a greater degree of power than any state has previously wielded in modern times.

10

Despite the concentration of power into the hands of a few states, the number of independent states in the world has increased rapidly in recent years, and so has disparity between their interests, their stages of social and political development and their conceptions of such things as international law. A plurality of states will still remain if some of today's states should succeed in amalgamating. If, indeed, they surmount the formidable obstacles which stand in the way of the amalgamation of separate states into one, as those of western Europe may conceivably do in time, it will be because they are determined to assert their place within an international system by combining to form a larger independent power.

In an international system the independent state is unable to abandon its primary concern with maintaining the security of its society and with advancing the interests of that society in competition with other states, if also by collaboration with them. No radical transformation of the modern international system followed upon the establishment of the United Nations Organisation. Since the United Nations Organisation is unlikely to be revitalised or superseded by the establishment of a single world state, no such transformation — one that would unanchor the system from its characteristic modes of operation, as these have evolved through time — is now to be expected. At least this side of an international catastrophe, problems in the international field will be problems confronting societies governed by independent states, and it will be by independent states, working in a system of states, that progress will be achieved if any is achieved.

Throughout history systems of states have proved to be inherently unstable. When we contemplate the chances of avoiding an international catastrophe, moreover, it is no consolation that the modern international system has been unstable in different ways from those which characterised the systems that preceded it. Before the end of the eighteenth century the resort to violence between states, as within them, was restrained by little but the limitation of resources and organisations and the need for recuperation when they had been exhausted. By the same token, destruction was limited: when violence was normal, catastrophe was highly localised. In the years since then the states that have formed the modern system have sought to make violence between themselves a matter of last resort, and their expanding capacity in resources and organisation has enabled them to be partially successful in avoiding it. But the expansion of their resources and their organisation have brought it about that their failures have produced progressively disastrous consequences on an ever-increasing scale.

When we look back on their failures — on the causes of modern wars — two generalisations may be made. As the lifetime of the modern international system has coincided with a continuing revolution in technology, with its profound impulse towards the better integration of societies and the greater efficiency of governments, so the serious changes in the distribution of power between themselves which its states have experienced have arisen from the uneven advance of this revolution in the different societies of which it has been composed. And states have exhibited a propensity to take risks or to believe that their calculations involved no risks when beset by the fear and uncertainty that have accompanied these changes. Some states may have been more prone than others to take risks or to ignore them. Greed and aggressiveness may have influenced states, as well as fear. Neither of these considerations need affect this general conclusion. One of two pre-conditions will have to be satisfied if the international system is to be kept stable in the future, as it has not been able to be kept in the past. States will either have to learn so to control technological growth and social and political change in a variety of societies that they can prevent serious changes from occurring, however slowly, in the international distribution of power. Or they will have to learn how to control themselves even when this distribution has become unstable.

It is not too much to add that they are unlikely to be able to make progress by the first of these routes. The balance of power rests on the relative strength of a large number of societies. When these relative strengths are linked not only to rapid technological change, but also to the way in which differences of social, governmental and cultural development vary the impact of this change from society to society, they will continue to lie beyond the resources of human management, and perhaps beyond accurate calculation. Those who concluded after the Second World War that the multi-lateral or kaleidoscopic quality had for ever been replaced by the unchallengeable hegemony of one super-power, or, later, by the bi-polar domination of two rival hegemonies, are already turning out to have been just as wrong as those who believed that international behaviour would be transformed by the principles of the United Nations Charter. If states are to avoid a further international catastrophe, then, it will be because they have learned to control themselves in unstable conditions.

Some transformation in international behaviour will be necessary if states are to succeed in doing this — a transformation more profound than any which has taken place since the beginning of the nineteenth century, when the modern international system was first set on its course. We cannot really doubt, indeed, that the modern international system has now at last come to a point in its development at which only one of two outcomes can ensue. Either it must undergo such a transformation or it will collapse completely.

The modern pattern of peace and war — that alternation of long periods of peace with short bursts of war which has characterised the modern international system — may be prolonged. The present period of peace may again be terminated by a return to war. In this case, not only will war be conducted, as it has always been conducted since the end of the eighteenth century, at a previously unparalleled level of violence and destruction, but also the level of destruction will indeed be catastrophic. Alternatively, the modern pattern may itself be terminated. That phase in the development of international relations which succeeded at the end of the eighteenth century to one in which warfare had been virtually continuous, but also limited in scale, may be succeeded in its turn by another phase — by one in which international relations would take their character from the fact that states had been driven to restrict their aims and to conduct their policies in such a way as to ensure that they stop short of the use of force between themselves.

Few of us can be unaware of the reason for this unprecedented situation. During the last half-century the power of technology and management to shorten distances and to change the character of societies and states has done nothing to brighten the prospects for the formation of a single world state. But between the more developed of the states it has finally brought about the development of war to that condition of inescapable mutual attrition at an insupportable level of destruction to which the increase in the scale of conflict and the deadliness of weapons has been driving inexorably since at least the 1870s.

It has done so by producing in these directions, in less than twenty years, an increase that dwarfs not merely all the expansion which took place between the 1870s and the Second World War, but all the expansion that took place in the whole of history before 1945. The atomic bomb of 1945 was a hundred times more destructive than the most deadly of previous weapons. The hydrogen bomb, introduced in the 1950s, was a thousand times more destructive than the atomic bomb. One aircraft could now deliver more explosive power than all the bombs dropped on Germany during the Second World War, and anything less than 100 per cent success in preventing aircraft from getting through air defences would have catastrophic results. And when such a degree of success had never previously been feasible, the replacement of aircraft by ballistic missiles, also in the 1950s, and then the perfection of the submarine as a moving missile-platform, rendered its attainment for ever impracticable.

Less widely understood, perhaps, are the rapidity with which governments have responded to this total and qualitative change in the armaments situation, and the extent to which they have done so. Occurring in the aftermath of the Second World War, it heightened the uncertainty, the strain and the rivalry that would in any case have accompanied the process of post-war resettlement, and thus contributed to the atmosphere of the Cold War. Despite this atmosphere, it not only provided them in their conduct of a series of crises with an overpowering immediate source of restraint in the last resort, but also produced a decisive shift in their conception of the function of military strategy.

In the unstable stage in the development of weapons which stretched from the 1870s to 1945 strategic thinking had already undergone one important change. Up to 1914 all strategic doctrines had one thing in common: the problem to be solved was the deployment of existing resources for the earliest possible decision in battle. Between 1918 and 1945 strategy had fallen into two schools. For one of them the First World War had sufficiently proved that war between developed states had become, not a matter of rapid decision by battle, but a prolonged and agonising process of attrition pending the total exhaustion of the vanquished society and involving the near-exhaustion of the victor side. Its adherents accordingly relied on the mobilisation of superior resources without regard to speed in their deployment. The other—and the more sophisticated—school held to the classical belief in the decisive battle, and continued to emphasise the lightning deployment rather than the maximum mobilisation of resources. They still hoped that with the aid of new weapons like the bomber and the tank, and of new techniques like the *blitzkrieg*, the horrors of deadlock and attrition could be mitigated, if not avoided. The doctrines of neither school could long survive in the nuclear age. No reliance could be placed on the mobilisation of superior resources when all the resources that could be used in war had to be ready in time of peace. When the essential resources were the hydrogen bomb and the capacity to deliver it, so that the attrition and destruction which had previously been prolonged for years would be effected in hours, it was no longer possible to save the concept of the decisive battle. Between nuclear states who were at each other's mercy the question, indeed, was whether it was possible to save the concept of war—to rescue war itself from obsolescence.

Even before the early 1950s men had spoken of the coming "balance of terror". As early as 1946 an American writer had heralded the day when military strategy would come to be pre-occupied not with waging war, but with avoiding it. "Thus far," he wrote, "the chief purpose of our military establishment has been to win wars. From now on its chief purpose must be to avert them. It can have almost no other useful purpose."[1] But it was in the early 1950s that the development of the hydrogen bomb, and the entry of Russia into the ranks of the states which possessed both the bomb and the capacity to deliver it at intercontinental ranges, drove governments to rely on the threat of massive nuclear retaliation to deter each other from risking war.

The doctrine of massive retaliation, of the great deterrent, was of course resisted. Groups which still hoped that war could be abolished by agreement or example—the Campaign for Nuclear Disarmament for example—opposed it, as they opposed the nuclear weapons themselves, as being immoral and obscene. Above all, however, strategic thinkers opposed it for the reason that by accepting the nuclear deadlock it also accepted a great reduction in the freedom of action of great powers in foreign policy.

Between 1956 and 1961 strategic studies developed into a major academic industry, especially in the United States. Most of the new recruits to it urged the replacement of "the great deterrent" by "a spectrum of deterrence" and of massive retaliation by "graduated" or "flexible" retaliation. Their declared purpose was to reintegrate strategy with foreign policy by providing a variety of military options for use in different international contingencies, and particularly for those contingencies in which the threat of massive retaliation would be "incredible" to another state, and in which the resort to it would be "unthinkable" for their own. For some of them, those for whom war between nuclear states had indeed been abolished by the nuclear stalemate, the main concern was to stress that conventional strategies would still be called for in conflicts with non-nuclear states, which the nuclear threat might not deter, or that the stalemate between nuclear states would still persist if the arms race were replaced by arms-limitation agreements. But the problem that preoccupied most of them, consciously or

[1] Brodie, B. (ed.) (New York, 1946), *The Absolute Weapon*, p. 76.

unconsciously, was how to preserve for the nuclear states the option of conducting limited wars between themselves.

Their fundamental assumption was that in a variety of ways — by maintaining conventional as well as nuclear forces; by developing small, or "tactical", nuclear weapons and missiles for use by ground troops; by extending the techniques of crisis management to embrace the rationing of nuclear exchanges — these states could recover the freedom to use the threat of war to influence each other. They could do this in the knowledge that in the event of war their conflict could remain conventional or that, if the war became nuclear, the escalation of their nuclear exchanges from one level to another could be controlled, and their mutual destruction thus restricted to supportable limits. Nor did the more extreme advocates of flexible or graduated response stop short of estimating in different numbers of millions of lives the different levels of destruction that might be acceptable in different contingencies or that might be avoided by different expenditures on civilian defence.

The nuclear deadlock withstood these disparate, and desperate, efforts to subvert it. Even had it been feasible, agreement on disarmament could not reverse the technological knowledge which produces the latest weapons and the means of delivering them, or guarantee that that knowledge would never be used to reproduce them. Massive obstacles prevented any government from adopting as confidently as did its more scholastic advisers the belief that war between nuclear states could be limited or its escalation controlled — and not least the impossibility of knowing whether the belief would be shared by other governments once war had broken out. Although some of the nuclear states went through the motions of accepting the strategy of flexible retaliation when the Cold War was at its height, and although they still retain some of the jargon and the trappings that go with it, they all resigned themselves during the 1960s to the facts. If provocation should lead to war — if, indeed, accident or miscalculation should do so — there was no reasonable hope of avoiding massive nuclear exchanges and no reasonable possibility of providing civil defence against them. And if it was thus imperative to avoid war, then, far from trying to avoid dependence on massive retaliation, it was no less imperative to ensure against provocation and miscalculation by seeing to it that, by possessing a second-strike nuclear force that would be invulnerable to a nuclear attack, all nuclear states should be able to rely on massive retaliation.

The acceptance of the nuclear deadlock in its modified form, in the doctrine of "the balance of deterrence", is now bringing the nuclear states slowly but surely to the point where, from being rivals in arms development, they are becoming partners in the task of maintaining the capacity to destroy each other, which technology has made available, as the only reliable method of preserving peace among themselves. It has already produced between them the development of new techniques of communication and surveillance and of new skills and precautions for the management of crises which constitute a revolution in diplomatic devices to keep pace with the revolution in weapons. Nor is there reason to doubt that, as well as agreeing that it is essential to do so, the states will find it easier to keep the balance of deterrence than it was to keep the balance of more conventional power that it has replaced.

They will continue to fear that the balance of deterrence might be upset by further technological advance. But no technological discovery is likely to remove the fundamental uncertainty on which it rests—is likely to guarantee to any state, however powerful, that it can avoid effective retaliation in the event that it attacks. The balance will be shaken from time to time as further states acquire the latest weapons and the means of delivering them, but it is unlikely to be more than temporarily shaken. Since she became a nuclear state, with the power to deliver nuclear missiles to the United States, Russia and Western Europe, China has been drawn into the single network of communication and restraint which the missiles impose on all states which possess them. Nor is it likely that any other new recruit to the ranks of these states could avoid being involved. The possibility that this network may not be proof against technical accident or psychological breakdown will theoretically remain ever-present. But the possibility is so obvious, and its consequences are so appalling, that the precautions of governments will make doubly sure that the network is as practically effective within each state as it is between states. In spite of all the dangers and uncertainties—on account of them, indeed—the recent decisive shift in the function of strategy and armaments will probably prove to be permanent.

The nuclear states—and not only they, for all the advanced states are now locked up together in a single system—have not only been brought by the revolution in weapons to the position we have already outlined. They know that they have been brought to it, and that for the first time in history they have no choice but to avoid uncontrollable violence by abstaining from further war between themselves.

At the same time as it has been bringing about a huge transformation in the techniques and the potential scale of war, the advance of technology and management on broader fronts— with its power to produce greater complexity within societies and greater integration between them, and thus to increase the variety of ways in which they can express their competitiveness and safeguard and increase their influence—has been depriving war of its rational purpose.

Throughout the history of the modern international system this effect has been at work, producing new forms of activity and new criteria of power, and ending the days when the spoils of war were the natural way of adding to a society's wealth. Until our own day, on the other hand, as well as always becoming uppermost once war has broken out and war-aims have begun to be defined, the calculation of material advantage has always played at least some part in the decision to resort to war. But the advanced societies are now coming to the point where, apart from being able to obtain no advantage whatever from war, but only damage and destruction, they have no rational objective which they cannot obtain more effectively by other means.

It is otherwise with the undeveloped and the under-developed societies of the world. To them, moreover, the nuclear deadlock does not extend and the nuclear deterrent cannot be applied. When we add that politically these societies are fundamentally unstable, it becomes difficult to resist the conclusion that another development of recent years must soon exert on the character of the international system an influence just as great, and in the same direction, as that of the balance of deterrence — the emergence of the backward societies into political independence and the fact that the advanced societies must in future co-exist with them.

In the years since the Second World War the leading states have handled this new problem with noticeable restraint. Despite the development of the atmosphere of cold war in the relations between themselves — despite the fact that the resulting tension has necessarily spilled over into the vacuum of the backward world, transforming what began as indigenous conflicts there into crises of major proportions — they have refrained from provoking each other during these crises, or have at least kept the provocation within bounds. The explanation is not far to seek. Great powers are no more able now than they were in the nineteenth century to prevent such conflicts. As a result of the vast increase in the number of new and unstable states it is probable, indeed, that they have become even less able to do so. But because they are in balance between themselves they are again able, as they were during much of the nineteenth century when confronting the Balkan question or scrambling for colonies, to prevent the resulting crises from involving them in war. Between the 1890s and 1939 their own balance was greatly disturbed and they had immense difficulty in containing crises, not to say in not manufacturing them. Ever since the end of the Korean War there has been for the opposite reason a steady increase in their determination to avoid extreme positions, as they have come to test and to understand in a series of confrontations the new balance which has been imposing itself upon them.

The new balance between them is novel in character, a balance of nuclear deterrence having superseded a balance resting on conventional criteria of power. As compared with the conventional balance, there is good reason for believing that, while it will not be self-regulating, it will be technically easier to maintain: the nuclear weapons have ushered in a new level of absolute power which reduces the significance of such changes in relative power as are bound to occur in a system of states. It will therefore be surprising if the Great Powers do not continue to tread with great caution when dealing with the undeveloped world. The very fact that this world might otherwise become an area of competitive intervention and predatory struggle between them will combine with the danger that any war between them will be a nuclear war to ensure that they will. Not for nothing do they now talk of their common fear that Israel will come to fill in the Middle East the role which Serbia performed in eastern Europe in 1914. It will be surprising, indeed, if they are not forced before long to recognise that caution is not enough, and that the problems of the undeveloped world, like the problem of maintaining the nuclear balance without incurring senseless and onerous expenditure, demand their positive collaboration.

Two courses lie before them. They might continue on the one they now follow, utilising disturbances in the backward societies jockeying for influence there through the supply of propaganda, arms and aid, exploiting the divisions of opinion which these disturbances produce throughout the international system, falling back on their power of veto in the Security Council, all with the aim of outwitting each other without driving each other to desperation. Alternatively, they might return to the forms and attitudes of the nineteenth-century Concert of Europe. By exerting their actual power to regulate these disturbances in close co-operation between themselves — better still by reactivating the Security Council, through which this actual power was for the first time invested by the terms of the United Nations Charter with legal authority and a constitutional base — they might establish a more continuous and extensive degree of co-operation than the nineteenth-century Concert was able to achieve.

They are unlikely to incur disastrous consequences if they persist in their present policies. One or another of the dramatic slides into chaos that are sure to be repeated in and between societies of the "third" world might one day coincide with some temporary dislocation of the nuclear balance between the modern states, and the coincidence might have the modern states at war with each other. In fact, this danger is no more real than is the prospect of any serious suspension of the nuclear balance itself. If they did exchange this course for that of collaboration, on the other hand, they would not solve the problems of the "third" world or prevent the convulsions to which those problems will give rise. All they could expect from establishing a framework for regulating the convulsions is that, by agreeing on spheres of influence or on joint interventions or on joint undertakings not to intervene, they could contain the consequences and hope to direct them into useful paths. For both of these reasons it may seem that it would be both pointless and burdensome for them to make the change, and idealistic to expect them to do so. But there are other considerations to be taken into account.

These are not the arguments which now lead demographers, ecologists, agronomists, economists, futurologists and even strategists to follow international lawyers and European inte-grationists in urging that the independent state and the process of diplomacy between independent states have become obstacles to the solution of the world's great problems, on the ground that in a world of shrinking distances, diminishing resources and increasing interdependence these problems are technical in character.

Between the 1860s and the Second World War technical problems first loomed large for the international system — part consequence and part cause of the movement of more complex societies towards closer contact and greater uniformity — and there was a huge proliferation of international technical arrange-ments — on explosives, prisoners of war, public health, patents, industrial conditions, postage, copyright and countless other subjects — for dealing with them. But this proliferation was accompanied not merely by the continuing insistence of govern-ments on their complete independence in political affairs, but also by a decline in the readiness of governments to collaborate for political ends. If it were the case that relations between the developed and the undeveloped societies involved only technical problems, we might be sure that this decline would not be reversed.

In reality, however, they are complicated by the most fundamental of all political issues, that of nationalism. Ever since they were transformed by a political process—the withdrawal of imperial control and its replacement by independent states— conditions in the undeveloped areas have been dominated by this issue. Ever since they had to adjust to this transformation the modern states have over-simplified the issue and misjudged its consequences. But it may be as much from contemplating the results as from accepting the balance of nuclear deterrence that, as well as taking care to avoid fighting about the undeveloped world, they have recently displayed more caution towards developments there.

In a world in which distances have been eliminated and technical and economic relations have become so close, the modern states reduce the instability of the backward areas by their mere existence alongside them. But it is this fact which has concealed the true condition of these areas—the full extent of the historical time-lag that separates them from the modern world. For all the disillusionment of recent years, the modern world has yet to learn an important lesson. These other states and societies cannot with their own resources quickly advance beyond their present stage of development and, however great its efforts, the modern world can do little to hasten their advance, the more so as it can no longer practise and no longer needs the methods of direct imperial control. The gap between the developed and the undeveloped societies is increasing, and not solely because, relatively, the developed world is undergoing rapid change. In at least some parts of the undeveloped world, conditions are deteriorating absolutely.

One reason for this is that, while it exerts some stabilising influence, their co-existence with a more sophisticated world is a source of confusion. It is not merely the case that the modern states have brought confusion to the backward world by their competition in propaganda and political intervention there. The modern societies have provided it with technologies and techniques which it cannot effectively use — except, as with modern armaments, for conducting war at a higher level of destruction than would otherwise have been possible or, as with modern means of communication, for creating and sustaining political emotions that would otherwise not exist or, as with modern public medicine, for producing increases of population which cannot be fed or employed. They have educated its governments to want programmes and to nurse aspirations which they cannot achieve and which thus drive them to frustration and despair. They have given it ideologies which it is unable to resist, but which are fundamentally irrelevant to its problems.

In the last resort, however, its instability derives from the historical and sociological stages of its development, and these external influences only exacerbate it. In both respects, its general condition bears some similarity to that which obtained in eastern Europe between the middle of the nineteenth century and 1939, when independent states succeeded to the empires of Turkey, Austria-Hungary and Russia. But there are two vital differences.

The eastern European empires were old-established, and they had for long maintained — they had indeed for long been intensifying — the effort to transform their societies into nation states. In the extra-European world the empires which have now withdrawn were recent and more alien structures, exercising a more superficial control. They have left to their successor states little of the bureaucratic momentum which enabled those of eastern Europe to persist in the nation-making work. These states have come into existence, moreover, in social conditions which resemble not those of even eastern Europe a century ago, but those of Europe before the sixteenth century, before its societies had undergone the first of successive waves of economic, technological, scientific and intellectual change. Throughout this area, to different extents because its development is at different stages, but in all cases to a greater extent even than in countries like Yugoslavia, the states are so new and so artificial, and the societies are so little removed from the ways of the tribe or the separatism of the culturally autonomous province, that no state is anchored to any society and no society to any state. The area lacks in any of its parts the necessary ingredients, political and social, either of an interstate system or of the modern nation.

The fact that the ideology of nationalism is a European importation is imperfectly grasped by those societies which have exported it. This has obscured the natural consequences of the situation. It has not greatly modified them. National movements in eastern Europe, at work in more developed societies and in opposition to centralising and nationalising states, resorted to the cultural or social concept of the political nation so long as they were in opposition. Not least because of the need to counter the tendency of the cultural sense of nationality to run to the extremes of pan-ism or tribalism, their leaders switched to the territorial or state concept of the political nation once the centralising empires had been overturned and they themselves had come to power. The main consequence of the more retarded social and political conditions of the extra-European world has been that its nationalist movements and its states have progressed—or drifted and deteriorated—in the reverse direction.

So long as they were movements of resistance to colonial empires, their aim was to take over the frontiers, the territory and the government institutions of the empire or colony in which they developed, and it was so necessarily. The movements were confined to elites, westernised by education or by involvement in the governmental or the economic activities of the ruling power, and aware that beyond their restricted memberships nationalism, and perhaps even the non-political sense of nationality, was non-existent. More than that, to have emphasised the cultural basis of the political nation, had that been possible, would have encouraged tribal separatism or cultural loyalties which transcended frontiers—sentiments which can command at least as much devotion as nationalism and which form the greatest obstacles to the creation of the political nation. When they succeeded to the power of the state, this remained their aim. In some respects the successor governments have fought for it with great tenacity, denouncing tribalism or communalism as treason and struggling to maintain the unity of their societies and the integrity of the frontiers that were bequeathed to them. But they have struggled against great odds. The natural tendency of the state to pursue the assimilation of different cultural groups within its territorial frame—to be an empire in relation to those groups—has been defeated or deflected by pressures which are no less powerful, and just as understandable in the circumstances.

These pressures spring from the excitement and the turmoil that have come with political independence. In one sense these have brought into existence the rival programme—the social, cultural or populist conception of the nation. To speak more accurately they have created a situation in which, even less than in eastern Europe during the nineteenth century, the cultural concept of the political nation is incapable of any consistent application when confronted by the rival claims of the tribe, the province, the territorial state, and the nationality that goes wider than the territory to be the vehicle to which it should be attached. In this situation the popular sense of nationality, so far as it has made any ground, wavers between the extremes of tribalism and pan-ism, but always carries the threat that it will combine with regional resentment and state inefficiency to produce civil war, as in Nigeria, or secession, as in East Pakistan, or the demand for decentralisation and federal autonomy which, as in the grievances now being expressed by the minority provinces of West Pakistan (Sind, Baluchistan and the North-West Frontier) against the dominant province (Punjab), may easily become the first step on the road to secession or at least to civil war. Nor is it surprising, in view of this constant threat, that the territorial state has been unable to avoid compromising with these pressures which contradict its fundamental objective of nurturing state nationalism and consolidating the territorial nation.

Unable to hold off the divisive forces within its territory, it has on the one hand given way to them. Hence the revision of the boundaries between India's sub-states on linguistic lines, following the original partition of the Indian sub-continent as far as possible in accordance with the wider communal divisions of religion and race; the massacres of Chinese in Indonesia and

11

Malaysia; the expulsion of "strangers" from Ghana; the expropriation of Asiatics and Europeans in east African states. Hence, also, the increasing extent to which in some African societies the establishment of the one-party state, originally a necessary device against the danger of tribal division, is yielding to the monopolisation of the single political party by one tribe or alliance of tribes, which uses the power of the state in its own interests and against those of other tribes.

On the other hand, the state has turned to pan-ism as an antidote to tribalism and other forms of separatism. Sometimes, as in the hands of President Nasser of Egypt, this policy has gone to the lengths of war and intervention against other states, imperialism within the state's frontiers being supplemented by imperialism beyond them, in neighbouring Arab societies. At other times it has produced the compromise by which separate territorial states have agreed to announce the federation of their culturally associated societies — Egypt and Syria; Tanganyika and Zanzibar; Egypt, Syria and Libya. More frequently it has been confined to rhetorical appeals on behalf of still weaker inter-state associations, like the Organisation for African Unity, or of still wider inter-community causes — pan-Arabism, pan-Negroism, pan-Africanism, or the even more ambitious programme which seeks to establish a single Muslim commonwealth of all Asian and African Islamic societies.

Where the state is new and unstable and the idea of the political nation, also new, fluctuates so easily between state nationalism and cultural nationalism, and between several possible frameworks in either case, the state can hardly omit these gestures of at least moral approval towards ideals and programmes which logically lead to its overthrow. In Latin America, in contrast, pan-continentalism has become a revolutionary movement against the states, as has pan-Turkism in Turkey: the states here have a longer history and are better established. It is not irrelevant that they are also either European in their ruling classes or that, in the case of Turkey, the ruling class represents the rump of an empire and not a colony which an empire has realised.

For confusion is deepened in the more backward societies of what were till recently European colonies, and the cement of political loyalty there is further diluted, by the powerful influence of racial sentiment and anti-European resentment. These sentiments provide most of the undeveloped world with a unity of emotion, if not always of action, which transcends its divisions of interest and culture, but which combines with its political weakness to retard its political development. Rejecting the West emotionally because of its imperial past, it is tempted also to reject the West's political experience, and particularly its evolution of the national political community, because of its own inability immediately to acquire the benefits of it.

Only if we recognise how these reactions reinforce each other can we understand the process by which African and Arab intellectuals have extended the ideology of nationalism beyond even its extreme pan-national cultural limits, and extracted from it, not a basis for political loyalty, but a justification for the doctrines of racism and anarchism. We have only to glance at these doctrines, on the other hand—at the "principle of racial sovereignty"; the conviction that intervention by one ex-colony in the affairs of another is not a violation of domestic jurisdiction, whereas any act of intervention by a developed state is an immoral exercise in imperialism; the dismissal as western or bourgeois hypocrisy of the idea that there can be aggression as between one African state and another or treason by a Nigerian on behalf of Ghana[1]—to recognise their significance. By their rejection of the legitimacy of the division of men into separate nations and states, they reflect the stunted development of nations and states in the backward world. But they can only delay the establishment there of this framework of political organisation and of the political loyalty which, while it has not avoided conflict, is the only framework on which conflict can be made productive and kept restrained.

Within this framework, relations between the state and society may vary from society to society. As the world's new political

[1] Mazrui, A. (1967), *Towards a Pax Africana.*

societies differ in the historical stage of their development, so they differ in the extent to which government can uphold the criteria of the nation which are associated with the state. In almost all of them, however, the dominant trend is towards cultural nationalism — or else towards the extremes of tribalism, pan-ism and racialism which lie beyond cultural nationalism and which are both its logical extensions and its antitheses. Perhaps the sole exception is provided by Israel.

Alone among the political societies founded since the Second World War, that of Israel was a product of cultural nationalism, not to say of a pan-national Zionist movement. It could not have been set up without the help of outside states, though it was finally achieved in defiance of them. It incorporated only a minority of Jews, though it had the sympathy of most of them. Despite these imperfections in its quality as a product of cultural nationalism, the Israeli state derives its unusual character from the fact that it has based national cohesion on cultural uniformity more completely, perhaps, than any state has previously been able to do. One illustration of this is the degree to which it has succeeded, where all similar efforts have failed, in reviving a dead script and making it, as Hebrew has been made, into a living and expanding vernacular language. Another may be found in its rule that Israeli nationality and Jewishness in religion, by the rabbinical definition of what is a Jew, must be inseparable. But despite these hallmarks of the culture-nation, it is now embarking upon transition towards the state-nation, or at least to greater emphasis on the state's criteria of the nation.[1]

In this respect, no less than in its original emphasis on the cultural nation, it is the exception among the new states. In this

---

[1] The mounting pressure for the registration as Jews by nationality of the children of mixed marriages, who are Gentiles by rabbinical law, is the first sign of recognition that divergence must develop between the Jewish culture-nation and the Israeli state-nation. In January 1970 the High Court of Justice overruled the Ministry of the Interior by authorising this registration, in modification of the rule which has been disputed since the creation of the state. For the present the High Court has itself been overruled by the Israeli government; but as Israel comes to incorporate non-Jews among its citizens, and as it develops the institutions and the outlooks of the modern state, with which it was also endowed from the outset, it will be surprising if it does not give increasing priority to the assimilation of its people and the integration of its territory.

respect, on the other hand, it begins to conform to the pattern established by development in the world's older political societies.

Where these had their origin in association with cultural nationalism, as in central Europe from the middle of the nineteenth century or in eastern Europe somewhat later, the turn towards the state criteria of the nation was not long delayed, even if the emotional appeal of politicised cultural affinity was not easily suppressed. If they had been established as state-nations before this appeal acquired its influence with the rise of mass participation in politics, as was the case in the West, the state criteria prevailed against it. The appeal was more than offset by the power of economic and technological change to bring about the greater integration of society and to expand society's need of the state. Even when men sought to supplant both the appeal of cultural nationalism and the function of the state by implementing the most nearly universal pan-ism of all times — the Marxist-Leninist vision of the withering away of all states in classless societies — they produced a more powerful state, and one which, taking over the multi-national society of the Russian Empire, has necessarily insisted on the state's criteria of the nation in its centralising work. More recently a state has itself driven one of the oldest and most conservative societies in the world through "the cultural revolution" against the state. But it has done so because this same vision is again fading fast in China after being transplanted there. At a time when China is at last emerging as one of the world's great states, moreover, the state has taken good care to insulate its essential apparatus — its nuclear installations, for example — against any harmful effects.

As well as varying from society to society, however, relations between state and society may change with circumstances within each society; and in most of the world's older societies it is now possible to discern a turn towards new forms of opposition to the state, and an increasing tendency to reject its claims.

It is possible to exaggerate this trend. Where the opposition takes the form of nationalist struggle against the state, as in Northern Ireland, Belgium or Spain, it represents the continuation or the revival of old cultural nationalisms which have withstood the process of assimilation. Where private violence for the purpose of influencing or overthrowing the state is used for other than nationalist causes, it similarly constitutes no completely novel development. If there has been a marked increase in the resort to this kind of violence since the end of the 1960s, it is not least because long-established revolutionary groups, long disillusioned by the increasing conservativism of Soviet Russia, felt their hopes revive with the cultural revolution in China, and judged that they might be advanced in the aftermath of the failure of the United States in Vietnam. But it will not have escaped the attention of governments in the older societies that cultural nationalism and other anti-state revolutionary movements, after being opposed to each other since the rise of Marxism, are beginning to join forces, or that both are deriving further strength from changes in the international and the domestic circumstances of these societies.

In the recent increase there of private civil violence – of the resort to force to influence the policy or overthrow the government of the state – some part has been played by the existence of old and perhaps ineradicable reservoirs of cultural national discontent and revolutionary or anarchical disposition, and some part, also, by the increasing tendency of cultural nationalist leaders to espouse anarchical doctrines, and of revolutionary groups to rush to the support of nationalist movements. But in the increasing variety of forms which the violence has assumed, rising from street demonstrations and student riots through politically-motivated strikes to the proportions, almost, of guerilla war, it is possible to detect the influence of other sources of disturbance, newer than nationalist or revolutionary discontent and more generally significant than the coming together of revolutionary and nationalist programmes. The rejection by the New Left of the materialism of modern society, a decade ago, foreshadowed the rise of a much broader discontent with the growing centralisation and standardisation of life and the increasing remoteness of the state. The contagiousness of violence has been increased by the technology of the modern world, which supplies dissent with dramatic techniques like television publicity and the device of aircraft hi-jacking, no less than by the fact that the older societies must co-exist with the backward world, which provides it with a constant supply of violent developments, confused doctrines and moral causes. And to these other reasons for the greater aggressiveness that is being brought to bear on internal political disagreements and social conflicts must be added another — the change that has come about in the public attitude in these societies to interstate war.

War everywhere retained a national function as well as some rational purpose as late as the Second World War. For all its growing destructiveness, for all the increasing reluctance to embark on it, it still brought adventure and significance to everyday lives when it occurred; and, by demanding great sacrifices, it still generated or re-generated social unity, provided it was conducted in a national cause. In societies like that of Israel, where a competent state and the basis of social unity exist, it retains this function. In most of the other new societies of the world it has not yet acquired it: the absence of social cohesion and of adequate state apparatus, which make it difficult to avoid, make it divisive in its effects. In the older and more advanced societies technological expansion has deprived war of its potential as a unifying and national force; and in a situation in which, far from being ultimately welcomed, war has come to be universally regarded as an absolute evil, at least if conducted between themselves, the individual need for adventure and the social reservoir of aggressiveness have been diverted into domestic confrontations.

It need not be expected that these new developments, with their divisive effects for the advanced societies, will result in the breakdown of the state. Still less will they lead to the disruption of the national political loyalty which, in such societies, necessarily rests (the more so the more they advance) on the intimate interdependence between a state and the bulk of the community. In some directions, indeed, they may ultimately lead to the strengthening of the powers of the state; the tightening of its relations with the community; the further de-tribalisation of nationalism to the point at which, when culture is cosmopolitan, only the state commands the loyalty which men will still need to give to the place and the arrangements in which they live. It cannot be expected, on the other hand, that the developments will die away. To these consequences of enormous changes in their material context, and to others which are sure to make their appearance, the advanced societies and states will have to adjust both their internal arrangements and the relations between each other.

The adjustment will not be a simple or a straightforward undertaking. Internally, the huge societies of Russia, China and the United States, the first nominally federal in structure, the second nominally unitary, and the third historically federal but increasingly approaching to a greater degree of centralisation, are all in their different ways already engaged with the same difficult problem—how to modify the centralisation that is inescapable in modern conditions by a degree of devolution of powers that falls short of the autonomy of classical federal theory, with its threat of separatism, but that will accommodate the increasing criticism of the state. If and when western Europe moves to greater integration between its separate societies, it will encounter this same problem in reverse. It will find that it is no less difficult to reconcile the resistance of local nationalisms and regional identities to its increasingly remote and cumbersome centralising activities, and that it is easier to propound novel formulae to this end—to state that the goal is to create "a nation made of nations", or a confederation which preserves the identity of the member nations, or a governing "Community" which is neither federal nor confederal in form—than it is to implement them.[1]

Internationally, the task facing these societies is just as complex. They have to adjust to the fact that their existence and

---

[1] For an indication of the contradictions that will arise—as also of the possibility that one of the effects will be what we have just referred to as the de-tribalisation of nationalism—see the recent plea from the President of the European Commission that EEC workers living in other Community countries than their own should have the right to vote in national elections there, on the ground that "all workers must be able to feel that they are at home in whatever Community country they are working and living". *The Times*, London, 25 April 1942.

security as separate societies, with all the divergences and rivalries which this entails, can be reconciled with instability in the undeveloped world and with the grave danger of instability nearer home, no less than with the nuclear deadlock, only if their divergences are contained and their rivalries are tempered by constructive exercises in collaboration. It is unlikely that this adjustment, any more than that which was forced on them by the nuclear weapons or that which is now being forced on them by domestic developments, will be completed without setbacks and delays. With it, too, the resort to novel formulae will prove to be of little assistance. But the formulae are being coined, and they at least indicate a mounting awareness of the fact that these inter-locking problems are also common problems, and that this adjustment to them must be made.

Fifteen years ago, when the Americans were perfecting the technical formula of the balance of deterrence, the government of Soviet Russia, more fertile in the field of ideological doctrine as it is more ingenious in its international political practice, gave birth to the theory of peaceful co-existence. It did so for two purposes. It had to convince itself that it was not abandoning the Marxist-Leninist laboratory of thought—and especially the belief that war is inevitable between capitalist and socialist societies—when in fact, after assessing the implications of the nuclear development, it was doing so. And then, having concluded that war between the great states had become impossible, but needing at the same time to perpetuate confrontation with the West in order to justify its demand for unity and discipline in Russia, it devised the theory to meet its hope that confrontation could continue unabated without involving the risk of war. There could be, and there must be, practical understanding between the governments of rival social systems, but between such systems purely ideological struggle must be maintained—this was what the theory laid down. But it is noticeable that in the past year or two this revisionist doctrine of co-existence has itself begun to be revised. In much the same way that strategic thinkers in the United States came to terms with the nuclear deadlock only after trying to escape it with the aid of theories of crisis management and limited war, the Russian authorities are now urging the West to respond to their wish for "a constructive approach to international relations" and the development of mutually advantageous ties by abandoning its attempts to sow dissension among the intellectuals, the young, and the various nationalities in Soviet Russia.[1]

They are, of course, also insisting that such attempts are damaging the policy of peaceful co-existence. But this need not conceal from us their growing recognition that the time has come when they should themselves lead the way in abandoning this policy, which after much initial indignation about its hypocrisy was accepted by the West for itself. Nor does this recognition come solely from learning that their indulgence in international ideological struggle may increase the internationalisation of civil violence to a point at which that threatens to produce repercussions at home. The policy of peaceful co-existence was most effectively and actively applied to the field of relations between the great states and the societies of the backward world. Until a few years ago the disposition of all the great states, and not of Russia alone, was to intervene in all the disturbances there. Ideologically, they were convinced that their own national interests were bound up with the outcome of its struggles and the conversion of its populations. In practical terms they did not doubt their ability to decide the outcome, and effect this conversion, without themselves coming to blows. More recently, however, they have acted with greater circumspection, and with some strange results.

Perhaps the earliest of these arose out of the Nigerian civil war. In this struggle the Soviet Union and Great Britain sustained the Federal government, while France, Portugal and South Africa supported secessionist Biafra, whose cause was also taken up by the European Left, and the United States remained aloof. The latest has occurred in East Pakistan, where Russia this time supported secession, the United States opposed it from consideration for the balance of power between China

[1] See the summary of a recent article by the deputy head of the KGB in the journal *Kommunist*, in *The Times*, London, 7 April 1972.

and Russia, and Great Britain stood aside. In between there was the spectacle of the United States, the Soviet Union and, after some hesitation, China all helping the government of Ceylon to crush a guerilla rising.

It is not unrealistic to see this transition, a transition from intervention in the cause of ideology and interest to intervention or abstention on grounds of interest alone, as resulting from a growing understanding that the unilateral and competitive handling of crises in the less-developed societies carries with it a further danger—that as well as producing repercussions in the older societies and contributing to the growth of violence and criticism there, it may serve only to deepen the serious instability of the backward world. In view of the obstacles that remain to be overcome, on the other hand, it would certainly be optimistic to expect it to be followed by the early establishment of an expanded Concert of the Great Powers for the better regulation of affairs in an expanded international system. Even if the other great states may be beginning to think along these lines, it will be some time before China can be brought to participate. But further explosions might well produce this further development, and if anything is certain it is that, in view of the political and social condition of the backward world, further explosions will take place.

Should this be the outcome, history will in one sense have repeated itself. Between 1815 and the 1830s the international system survived a series of crises involving the clash of material interests between individual states and ideological differences between two groups of states which were not unlike those which have occurred since 1945. In the course of these crises the leading states evolved the practical procedures of the Concert system which, in that they were prosaic alongside the more ambitious theory of the Holy Alliance and yet arose from the same anxiety to avoid war, were equivalent to those devices which today's leading states have developed alongside the United Nations Organisation as the necessary means of controlling their possession of nuclear weapons. With the aid of these procedures they came to recognise that a balance prevailed between them and thus to be able to use the Concert to help them to avoid extreme policies and to collaborate in the face of common problems. Not the least of these problems, then as now, arose from the spread of nationalism beyond their own borders and the increase of disorder, and the fear of revolution, within their own societies. Should this parallel be completed in what remains of the twentieth century, between greater states and on a larger geographical scale, it will be neither surprising nor particularly significant. In recent years the signs have multiplied to the effect that confrontation has for the present had its day. In the conditions of the modern international system the emphasis can only shift between confrontation and collaboration.

Of considerably greater significance is the fact that the first Concert system was unable to survive the strains which preceded the First World War. To set up a second will not be easy; but to set up a second that will not collapse in its turn—to ensure that history does not thus far repeat itself—will be an undertaking of far greater difficulty. We cannot be confident that men in the future will be more successful with it than they have been in the past. But reflection on the history of the modern international system might increase their interest in making the attempt. By emphasising how the processes which produced that system in the first place have already completed, in so short a time as the period since the Second World War, changes in the character of their societies and of their international circumstances which are more profound than any which men have ever previously experienced, it might indeed convince them, for the first time, that they cannot allow their efforts to fail.

BIBLIOGRAPHY

(1) *Nationalism*

The two standard bibliographies on nationalism are K. Pinson, *Selected Bibliography on Nationalism*, (New York, 1935) and K. W. Deutsch, *Interdisciplinary Bibliography on Nationalism, 1935–1953*, (M.I.T., 1956). Since the second of these was published there has been an enormous increase in the already large literature on the subject. This is partly because, as its title already recognised, the newer disciplines, especially sociology, have begun to concern themselves with a subject which was previously the preserve of historians and political scientists, and partly because a subject which was previously studied mainly in its European context has claimed the attention of the expanding body of scholars and students who are concerned with developments in the rest of the world.

The most recent guide to the latest literature is Anthony D. Smith, *Theories of Nationalism* (London, 1971). This is also the best general introduction to the subject in that, though the work of a sociologist, it classifies and criticises contributions from all the disciplines.

Other general books may be divided into two categories. Those which deal mainly with the formation of the nation and of national consciousness tend to be written by sociologists. They include:

B. Akzin, *State and Nation* (London, 1964).

K. W. Deutsch, *Nationalism and Social Communication* (2nd edn., New York, 1966).

E. Gellner, *Thought and Change* (London, 1964).

M. Ginsburg, *Nationalism, A Reappraisal* (Leeds, 1961).
L. Lefur, *Races, Nationalités, Etats* (Paris, 1922).
D. Lerner, *The Passing of Traditional Society* (New York, 1964).

To these may be added:

L. Doob, *Patriotism and Nationalism* (New Haven and London, 1964)
and

F. Hertz, *Nationality in History and Politics* (London, 1964), which discuss or advance psychological explanations of the formation of the nation;
H. G. Johnson (ed.), *Economic Nationalism in Old and New States* (London, 1968), which covers the relationship between national consciousness and economic policies; and
J. A. Fishman *et al.* (eds.) *Language Problems of Developing Countries* (New York, 1968)
and

R. B. Le Page *The National Language Question* (London, 1964), which deal with the linguistic complications.

The second category of general books is more concerned with concepts of the nation and with the historical development of nationalism as an ideology, and the books are mainly by historians and political scientists. The leading works here are:

A. Cobban, *The Nation State and National Self Determination* (London, 1969).
C. J. S. Hayes, *The Historical Evolution of Modern Nationalism* (New York, 1931).
E. Kedourie, *Nationalism* (London, 1960).
H. Kohn, *The Idea of Nationalism* (New York, 1967).
H. Kohn, *Nationalism, Its Meaning and History* (Princeton, 1955).
C. A. Macartney, *National States and National Minorities* (London, 1934).
K. Minogue, *Nationalism* (London, 1967).
Royal Institute of International Affairs, *Nationalism, A Report* (London, 1939).

B. C. Schafer, *Nationalism, Myth and Reality* (New York, 1955).

H. Seton-Watson, *Nationalism, Old and New* (London, 1965).

L. Snyder, *The Meaning of Nationalism* (New Brunswick, 1954).

I. Zangwill, *The Principle of Nationality* (London and New York, 1917).

Among more specialist books, by far the greatest number are case-studies of nationalism at particular periods and in particular areas. The following small selection lists some of the work which concentrates on recent and contemporary nationalism. The only attempt at a comprehensive survey of this field, L. Snyder, *The New Nationalism* (Ithaca, 1968), is somewhat superficial in its classification of post-1945 nationalisms by regional and other secondary divergences, rather than by the basic stages of political and social development. On the other hand, attempts to go beyond what these basic stages will permit, and to construct a more elaborate sociological classification of types of nationalism, are scarcely more successful in dispersing the first impression that may be gained from these case-histories, which is that every manifestation of nationalism is *sui generis*.

L. Binder, *The Ideological Revolution in the Middle East* (New York, 1964).

J. Bracey *et al.* (eds.), *Black Nationalism in America* (Indianapolis and New York, 1970).

J. S. Coleman, *Nigeria: Background to Nationalism* (Berkeley, 1958).

R. Conquest, *Soviet Nationalities Policy in Theory and Practice* (London, 1967).

P. H. Gulliver (ed.), *Tradition and Transition in East Africa* (London, 1969).

S. Haim, *Arab Nationalism* (Berkeley, 1962).

B. Halpern, *The Idea of the Jewish State* (Cambridge, 1961).

C. Heimsath, *Indian Nationalism and Hindu Social Reform* (Princeton, 1964).

A. Hertzberg, *The Zionist Idea* (New York, 1960).

T. Hodgkin, *Nationalism in Colonial Africa* (London, 1956).

M. B. Jansen, *Changing Japanese Attitudes to Modernisation* (Princeton, 1965).

H. Kohn, *American Nationalism: An Interpretative Essay* (New York, 1957).

B. Lewis, *The Emergence of Modern Turkey* (2nd edn., London, 1968).

J. M. Lonsdale, "Some Origins of Nationalism in East Africa", in *Journal of African History*, IX, 1 (1968), pp. 379ff.

E. S. Munger, *Afrikaner and African Nationalism* (London, 1967).

Victor Purcell, *The Chinese in South-East Asia* (London, 1964; new edn.).

R. Rotberg, "African Nationalism, Concept or Confusion?" in *Journal of Modern African Studies*, IV, 1 (1967), pp. 33ff.

R. Schlesinger, *The Nationalities Problem and Soviet Administration* (London, 1956).

A. Seal, *The Emergence of Indian Nationalism* (Cambridge, 1968).

R. Storry, *The Double Patriots: A Study of Japanese Nationalism* (London, 1957).

A. P. Whitaker and D. C. Jordan, *Nationalism in Contemporary Latin America* (New York, 1966).

The problem of where to draw the line between nationalism and, on the other hand, tribalism and other forms of pre-national political loyalty is raised by some of the foregoing works, notably those by Gulliver (the article by W. J. Argyle entitled "European Nationalism and African Tribalism"), Hodgkin, Lonsdale and Rotberg. The associated problem of pan-ism is dealt with in:

S. G. Inman, *Problems in Pan-Americanism* (New York, 1922).

C. Legum, *Pan-Africanism* (London, 1962).

H. Kohn, *Panslavism* (2nd. edn., New York, 1960).

J. B. Lockley, *Pan-Americanism. Its Beginnings* (New York, 1920).

Ali Mazrui, *Towards a Pax Africana* (London, 1967).

A. Reid, "Nineteenth Century Pan-Islam in Indonesia and Malaysia" in *Journal of Asian Studies*, 26, 2 (1967), pp. 267ff.

M. Wertheimer, *The Pan-German League, 1890–1914* (New York, 1924).

P. Worsley, *The Third World* (London, 1964).

S. Zenkovsky, *Pan Turkism and Islam in Russia* (Cambridge, Mass., 1960).

The relationship between nationalism and fascism and between nationalism and socialism raises issues which, though in some respects an extension of those connected with pan-ism, also involve other considerations. For its relationship with fascism see:

H. Arendt, *The Origins of Totalitarianism* (London, 1958).

M. D. Biddiss, "Fascism and the Race Question", in *Race*, X, (1968–69), pp. 251ff.

G. L. Mosse, "The Genesis of Fascism", in *Journal of Contemporary History*, I, 1 (1966), pp. 14ff.

H. Seton-Watson, "Fascism, Right and Left", in *Journal of Contemporary History*, I, i (1966), pp. 183ff.

S. J. Woolf (ed.), *The Nature of Fascism* (London, 1968).

For its relationship with socialism see:

W. M. Ball, *Nationalism and Communism in South-east Asia* (New York, 1952).

H. B. Davis, *Nationalism and Socialism* (New York and London, 1967).

J. H. Kautsky (ed.), *Political Change in Undeveloped Countries* (New York, 1962).

Ivo Lapenna, *State and Law: Soviet and Yugoslav Theory* (London, 1964).

R. Pipes, *The Formation of the Soviet Union: Communism and Nationalism, 1917–1923* (Cambridge, Mass., 1955).

S. Shaheen, *The Communist Theory of Self-Determination* (The Hague, 1956).

(ii) *The International System*

No attempt is made here to suggest books dealing mainly with the detailed diplomatic history of international relations. This may be studied in standard works such as the *New Cambridge Modern History* and P. Renouvin (ed.), *Histoire des Relations*

12

Internationales, to which may be added A. J. P. Taylor, *The Struggle for Mastery in Europe* (Oxford, 1954), for the years from 1848 to 1918 and, for the twentieth century, F. S. Northedge and M. J. Grieve, *A Hundred Years of International Relations* (London, 1971) and Peter Calvocoressi, *World Politics since 1945* (London, 1968).

Among the books dealing more generally with the history of the modern international system, including the development of attitudes to international relations, the following are broad surveys:

Adda B. Boseman, *Politics and Culture in International Relations* (Princeton, 1960).

Gaston Bouthoul, *Huit Mille Traités de Paix* (Paris, 1948).

Lord Bryce, *International Relations* (London, 1922).

Herbert Butterfield, *Christianity, Diplomacy and War* (London, 1953).

Herbert Butterfield and Martin Wight (eds.), *Diplomatic Investigations* (London, 1966).

C. R. M. F. Crutwell, *A History of Peaceful Change in the Modern World* (London and New York, 1937).

Ludwig Dehio, *Precarious Balance: The Politics of Power in Europe, 1944–1945* (London, 1963).

E. M. Earle (ed.), *Nationalism and Internationalism* (New York, 1950).

M. G. Forsyth, H. A. M. Keens-Soper and P. Savigear, *The Theory of International Relations: Selected Texts from Gentili to Treitschke* (London, 1970).

F. H. Hinsley, *Power and the Pursuit of Peace* (Cambridge, 1963).

T. J. Lawrence, *The Society of Nations, Its Past, Present and Possible Future* (Oxford, 1919).

F. Meinecke, *Machiavellism* (London, 1957).

Hans Morgenthau, *Politics among Nations* (New York, 1960).

A. Nussbaum, *A Concise History of the Law of Nations* (revised edn., New York, 1954).

P. Renouvin and J. B. Duroselle, *Introduction to the History of International Relations* (London, 1968).

F. M. Russell, *Theories of International Relations* (New York, 1936).

F. L. Schuman, *International Politics. An Introduction to the Western State System* (New York, 1941).

F. M. Stawell, *The Growth of International Thought* (London, 1929).

The above may be supplemented by a selection from works which, though dealing with specialist topics or restricted periods, bear on the general development of the international system:

M. S. Anderson, "18th Century Theories of the Balance of Power", in M. S. Anderson and Ragnhild Hatton (eds.), *Studies in Diplomatic History . . . in memory of D. B. Horn* (London, 1970).

A. C. F. Beales, *The History of Peace* (London, 1931).

E. H. Carr, *Nationalism and After* (London, 1945).

Gordon Craig and Felix Gilbert (eds.), *The Diplomats, 1919–1939* (Princeton, 1963).

Ludwig Dehio, *Germany and World Politics in the 20th Century* (London, 1959).

Felix Gilbert, *To the Farewell Address: Ideas of Early American Foreign Policy* (Princeton and Oxford, 1961).

L. Fischer, *The Soviets in World Affairs* (2 vols., 2nd edn., Princeton, 1951).

Denys Hay, *Europe, The Emergence of an Idea* (Edinburgh, 1957).

F. H. Hinsley, *Sovereignty* (London and New York, 1966).

C. Holbraad, *The Concert of Europe: A Study in German and British International Theory, 1815–1914* (London, 1970).

I. C. Y. Hsü, *China's Entrance into the Family of Nations . . . 1858–1880* (Cambridge, Mass., 1960).

George Kennan, *American Diplomacy, 1900–1950* (Chicago, 1951).

George Kennan, *Russia and the West under Lenin and Stalin* (London and Boston, 1961).

G. Mattingly, *Renaissance Diplomacy* (London, 1955).

P. E. Moseley, *The Kremlin and World Politics* (New York, 1960).

Harold Nicolson, *Diplomacy* (3rd edn., Oxford, 1963).

Robert E. Osgood, *Ideals and Self-interest in American Foreign Policy* (Chicago, 1953).

W. A. Phillips, *Confederation of Europe* (London, 1914).

Albert Sorel, *Europe and the French Revolution: The Political Traditions of the Old Regime* (London, 1969).

E. Souleyman, *The Vision of Peace in 17th and 18th Century France* (Columbia, 1942).

C. K. Webster, *The Congress of Vienna* (London, 1934).

C. K. Webster, *The Art and Practice of Diplomacy* (London, 1961).

From an enormous literature on the League of Nations and the United Nations the following is a small selection:

S. D. Bailey, *The General Assembly of the United Nations* (London, 1964).

J. L. Brierly, *The Covenant and the Charter* (Cambridge, 1947).

D. C. Coyle, *The United Nations and How it Works* (London and New York, 1967).

R. Higgins (ed.), *United Nations Peacekeeping* (2 vols., London, 1969).

H. G. Nicholas, *The United Nations as a Political Institution* (London, 1967).

A. F. Pollard, *The League of Nations in History* (London, 1919).

W. E. Rappard, *The Quest for Peace since the World War* (Cambridge, Mass., 1940).

J. T. Shotwell and M. Salvin, *Lessons on Security and Disarmament: From the History of the League of Nations* (New York, 1949).

F. P. Walters, *A History of the League of Nations* (London, 1952).

C. K. Webster and S. Herbert, *The League of Nations in Theory and Practice* (London, 1933).

On war Quincy Wright, *A Study of War* (Chicago and London, revised edn., 1964) is the most comprehensive analysis in English. It may be supplemented by the following books on the history of war:

Raymond Aron, *The Century of Total War* (London, 1954).

Raymond Aron, *War and Industrial Society* (London, 1958).

James A. Brundrage, *Medieval Canon Law and the Crusader* (Madison, Milwaukee, and London, 1969).

Sir George Clark, *War and Society in the 17th Century* (Cambridge, 1958).

Sir Charles Oman, *A History of the Art of War: The Middle Ages from the 4th to the 14th Century* (2 vols., 2nd edn., London, 1924).

Sir Charles Oman, *A History of the Art of War in the 16th Century* (London, 1937).

R. A. Preston, S. F. Wise and H. O. Werner, *Men in Arms: A History of Warfare and its Interrelationships with Western Society* (New York, 1956).

Theodor Ropp, *War in the Modern World* (Durham, N. Carolina, and London, 1959).

R. C. Smail, *Crusading Warfare* (Cambridge, 1956).

T. F. Tout, *Medieval and Modern War* (Manchester, 1919).

A. Vagts, *A History of Militarism* (Cleveland, USA and London, 1959).

and by the following works, which are valuable as either introducing or summarising the immense literature on war, strategy and weapon-control that has been produced by the introduction of nuclear weapons and other recent technological developments:

Raymond Aron, *Peace and War among Nations* (London, 1964).

Raymond Aron, *The Great Debate* (New York, 1964).

Ivan Bloch, *The Future of War in its Technological Economic and Political Relations* (Boston, 1902).

G. Bouthoul, *Les Guerres* (Paris, 1950).

Alastair Buchan, *War and Modern Society* (London, 1966).

F. W. Hirst, *The Political Economy of War* (London, 1915).

Michael Howard, *Studies in Peace and War* (London, 1970).

Robert E. Osgood and Robert W. Tucker, *Force, Order and Justice* (Baltimore, 1967).

A. C. Pigou, *The Political Economy of War* (London, 1921).

K. N. Waltz, *Man, The State and War* (New York, 1959).

For recent developments and controversies in the field of international law:

D. W. Bowett, *The Law of International Institutions* (London, 1964).

J. L. Brierly, *The Law of Nations* (several editions).

S. Prakash Sinha, *New Nations and the Law of Nations* (Leyden, 1967).

C. W. Jenks, *The World beyond the Charter in Historical Perspective* (London, 1969).

Georg Schwarzenberger, *International Law and Order* (London, 1971).

J. H. W. Verzijl, *International Law in Historical Perspective* (4 vols., Leyden, 1968).

Charles de Visscher, *Theory and Reality in Public International Law* (Princeton and London, 1957).

The above list represents but an introduction to a huge literature on international law, and the same applies to the following selection of books analysing or reflecting on political developments in international relations since the Second World War:

Coral Bell, *The Conventions of Crisis* (London, 1971).

Alastair Buchan (ed.), *Europe's Futures, Europe's Choices* (London, 1969).

A. L. Burns, *Of Powers and Their Politics* (Englewood Cliffs, 1968).

Peter Calvocoressi, *World Order and New States* (London, 1964).

M. Camps, *European Unification in the Sixties* (London, 1966).

S. C. Easton, *The Rise and Fall of Western Colonialism* (London, 1964).

R. Gartoff, *Soviet Strategy in the Nuclear Age* (New York, 1962).

E. B. Haas, *Beyond the Nation-State* (Stanford, 1964).

J. H. Hertz, *International Politics in the Atomic Age* (New York, 1959).

C. Holbraad (ed.), *Super Powers and World Order* (Canberra, 1971).

Institute for Strategic Studies, *Civil Violence and the International System* (Adelphi Papers 82 and 83, London, 1971).

M. A. Kaplan (ed.), *The Revolution in World Politics* (New York, 1962).

Henry A. Kissinger, *American Foreign Policy: Three Essays* (New York, 1969).

U. Kitzinger, *The European Common Market and Community* (London, 1967).

W. Laqueur and L. Labedz, *Polycentrism: the New Factor in International Politics* (London and New York, 1962).

George Liska, *Nations in Alliance* (Baltimore, 1962).

George Liska, *Imperial America: The International Politics of Primacy* (Baltimore, 1967).

William V. O'Brien (ed.), *The New Nations in International Law and Diplomacy* (London, 1965).

E. F. Penrose, *The Revolution in International Relations* (London, 1965).

John Strachey, *On the Prevention of War* (London, 1962).

Kenneth Thompson, *Political Realism and the Crisis of World Politics* (Princeton, 1960).

K. J. Twitchett and C. Cosgrove, *The New International Actors* (London, 1970).

Arnold Wolfers, *Discord and Collaboration* (Baltimore, 1962).

Index

DATE DUE

NOV 1 6 78			
GAYLORD			PRINTED IN U.S.A.